GUINNESS

MORE

SOCCER

SHORTS

JACK ROLLIN
Illustrations by David Arthur

GUINNESS PUBLISHING

Editor: Charles Richards
Design: Kathleen Aldridge
Illustrator: David Arthur

Copyright © Jack Rollin 1991

The right of Jack Rollin to be identified as the Author of this Work has
been asserted in accordance with the Copyright, Design & Patents Act 1988.

Published in Great Britain by Guinness Publishing Ltd, 33 London Road,
Enfield, Middlesex

Typeset in Palatino and Futura by Ace Filmsetting Ltd,
Frome, Somerset

Printed and bound in Great Britain by The Bath Press, Bath, Avon

"Guinness" is a registered trademark of Guinness Publishing Ltd

A catalogue record for this book is available from the British Library.

ISBN 0–85112–992–7

Readers of *Soccer Shorts* will recall how Jack Rollin, having turned down Chicago Maroons' offer of a trial as a centre-forward, then had to take over as a goalkeeper when Leon (A Funny Thing Happened on the way to the Forum) Greene furthered his operatic and film career. Pictured above in an Essex Junior Cup-tie, Jack prepares to clear his lines, covered by two well-placed defenders.

Twice bombed out in three days during the London blitz and strafed by a German plane while on the beach at Teignmouth when evacuated, Jack's service in the RAF during the Korean War was much more peaceful. He claims to have served three monarchs: King George VI, Queen Elizabeth II and Queen Juliana of Holland during a week's guard of honour.

While stationed at Fighter Command HQ at Bentley Priory, a late night once left him slow to respond to the Orderly Sergeant's early morning call. Thinking quickly, he said he was reporting sick with cartilage trouble and was sent to a specialist. Much to his and the NCO's surprise, cartilage trouble was indeed diagnosed!

At the age of 38, having retired some years earlier with ankle ligament problems, he was honoured by being invited to play in a friendly against the Greek champions Panathinaikos three days before their European Cup Final against Ajax at Wembley. He wisely declined. The team lost 15–0 . . .

CONTENTS

SPECIAL FEATURES

GUNNERS IN REVERSE ORDER ● DON'T JUST SAY
BROWN ● TEN YEARS ON ● FOOTBALL AND
FISHING ● SPECTATOR SEES MOST OF THE ACTION
● SUPPORT YOUR LOCAL TEAM ● RESTRICTED
OUTPUT ● FEAST OF FOOTBALL ● MOST
EXPENSIVE TEAM ● FOOTBALL LEAGUE OF
NATIONS ● BLANK VERSE

REWRITING HISTORY

Ageing manuscripts discovered in the Unnatural Science Museum have revealed many important historical events in the evolution of football:

Stonehenge was the original site of goalpost manufacture . . . Roman Baths were the first Football Pools . . . The Normans introduced the collection of taxes to aid poor clubs. It was known as the Levy Plan . . . First tourists were the Crusaders. But at home Prince John attempted to take over the English League. His moves were opposed by Nottingham Forest and he was eventually suspended for life by the Management Committee (Magna Carta) . . . William Caxton printed the first football programmes . . . In 1611 Baronets were introduced to stop the ball when a goal was scored . . . William of Orange invented the half-time refreshment . . . An American tour in 1774 was a disaster, chiefly due to the use of German guest players . . . The Duke of Wellington invented the continental lightweight boot . . . Among many outstanding French players was Napoleon Bonaparte. The French sportspaper *La Bastille* once headlined: Napoleon remains transferred to Paris . . . Thomas a'Bucket was the first trainer . . . Watt was the first player sent off for a current offence . . . Voltaire was an electrifying striker, Karl Marx the greatest left-winger . . . An English touring team in India had problems; the defence was split time after time by the Khyber Pass . . . Jules Verne wrote the first football book called *Twenty Thousand Leagues under the Sea* . . . During a long, boring tour of South Africa in 1898, matches at Ladysmith and Mafeking went into extra time.

The Druids' Dodgykikus takes the vital kick against the Cannibals' formidable goalkeeper Ug in the Stone Age Cup Final penalty shoot-out

ODDBALLS

NII NIL POINTS
Anderlecht's Ghanaian striker Nii Odartey Lamptey was 16 on 10 December 1990, but had already made a sensational start to his League career in Belgium, scoring in each of his first four games. Then in the UEFA Cup on 20 March 1991 his 82nd minute goal against Roma made him the youngest marksman ever in any European cup competition.

VIVE LA DIFFERENCE
A professional is a man who can play well when he doesn't want to play at all: an amateur is a man who would like to play well but can't.

WOOL CITY'S YOUTHFUL MEMORIES
When Bradford Park Avenue appointed Ken Roberts their trainer coach in 1967 it produced an unusual coincidence. His League debut as a Wrexham amateur inside-forward on 1 September 1951 was on Bradford's ground. He was 15 years 158 days old at the time, exactly the same age as Albert Geldard when he made his debut for Bradford against Millwall in Division Two on 16 September 1929.

FROM DESTITUTION TO DOLEMAN
The world's two oldest football clubs, Hallam and Sheffield, first met in 1862 to raise funds for destitute Lancashire mill workers. On 2 January 1988 a 125th anniversary match was staged, though it was in fact a specially arranged County Senior League Division One fixture to coincide with the charity match's commemoration. Hallam won 8–0, winger Mark Walshaw scoring six goals, Bob Doleman scoring the other two.

INITIAL TRAINING
Wilf Dixon's first club was Silksworth IOGT – Independent Order of Good Templars, open only to teetotallers. Dixon turned professional with Aldershot in pre-war days and subsequently acted as trainer to them and later Southend United. He also became coach and assistant manager to several other clubs including Tottenham Hotspur and Arsenal.

NOT SO SLOW BURNS
In October 1921 Jack Burns was sent off on his League debut for Rochdale.

FORFAR FROM HOME
The first Forfar Athletic player to become a professional was left-back Adam Ogilvie when he was signed by Grimsby Town in 1888. He subsequently made 38 League and Cup appearances for the Mariners once they had entered the League in 1892.

OLD BOYS REUNION
Hamilton Academical are the only senior club in Great Britain named after a school (Hamilton Academy). They have been based on the west side of the town since 1888, the year the club became a professional outfit.

HUGH THE TRIALIST
Hughie Gallacher once played in a trial game for Queen of the South in January 1921 scoring four times in a 7–0 win over St Cuthbert Wanderers.

PRIOR DONS
Long before Aberdeen became known as the Dons, they were first called the Whites then the Wasps.

TYNECASTLE TOMMY
The honour of scoring the first goal at home for Hearts in 1890 went to Tommy Jenkinson in a 4–1 friendly win over Bolton Wanderers.

GOAL AND GAOL
St Johnstone's first ground was the Recreation Ground opposite Perth Prison. It was opened on 15 August 1885 with a game between Scottish Cup holders Queen's Park and Dundee's Our Boys.

KING KENNY
On 3 May 1986 a goal by Kenny Dalglish for Liverpool at Chelsea clinched the League Championship. It was his first season as manager.

MAC THE STRIFE (1)
Peter McConnell left school at 15 to join Leeds United in 1952 under manager Major Frank Buckley. After two weeks at Leeds during which he was involved in training routines, he had not kicked a ball once. When he went to collect his wages, he was told he was being sent home. McConnell protested furiously, pointing out he had been given no chance to show his ability. His pleas resulted in him being kept on. One day while acting as a linesman in a practice match between the first team and the reserves, one wing-half was injured and McConnell took over. He soon won an 'A' team place, and stayed eight seasons before moving to Carlisle United and Bradford City.

MAC THE STRIFE (2)
John McClelland was a youngster in the Portsmouth area. He received a postcard requesting him to play for Manchester City's fifth team. Arriving at the ground he discovered another lad had been given his place. Disappointed, he complained to his father Jimmy who was on the City coaching staff. He was able to make arrangements for his son to have an 'A' team game and the lad was subsequently signed as a professional in March 1953, later playing for Lincoln City, Queen's Park Rangers, Portsmouth and Newport County.

WHO DARES LOSES
When the Football League was formed in 1888 it was agreed that the home teams would pay visiting clubs £12 out of gate receipts. West Bromwich Albion wanted only wins (2 points) to count in the League table.

LONG-VIEW VILLA
Aston Villa players scored the first two longest-distance headed goals in Football League games. Frank Barson did so from 30 yards against Sheffield United on Boxing Day 1921 and Peter Aldis achieved his feat from 35 yards against Sunderland on 1 September 1952.

BARRING ACCIDENTS

In 1956 a game at Salta, Argentina, between inmates of the local prison and an outside team ended in a free-for-all when two of the inmates recognised one of the outsiders as a police officer and attacked him. In the same year five long-term prisoners in Parkhurst qualified as football referees.

UNUSUAL ORIGINS

Bristol Rovers were known as the Black Arabs and wore black shirts . . . Chelsea were turned down by the Southern League before gaining admission to the Football League . . . The Alexandra of Crewe came from the pub where meetings were first held . . . Doncaster's first game was against the Yorkshire Institution for the Deaf . . . Liverpool was formed after the majority of Evertonians quit Anfield for Goodison Park in 1892 . . . Middlesbrough came into being at a tripe supper . . . Millwall were formed by workers in a local jam and marmalade factory . . . Norwich's founders met at the Criterion Cafe . . . the Torquay prime movers were local school old boys, the idea coming while listening to the band . . . Wigan Athletic started at a public meeting at the Queen's Hotel.

'I knew I should have shaved my moustache off!'

Have boots will travel – one of the few to get his kicks from the Job Centre

MANPOWER SERVICES

Jim Furnell applied to the Labour Exchange for work, enquiring whether he could become a footballer. He went to Burnley and eventually turned professional there in November 1954. Later he played for Liverpool, Arsenal, Rotherham United and Plymouth Argyle, making well over 400 League appearances as a goalkeeper.

Les Allen had a similar experience and was sent to West Ham United for a trial, but after half a game was told to come back in two years. Meanwhile he played for Briggs Sports, while acting as a storeman in the car factory. At 17, in September 1954, Chelsea signed him and he later played for Tottenham Hotspur and Queen's Park Rangers scoring over 100 League goals and winning England Under-23 and Football League representative honours.

DOUBLE FIRST

The first World Cup match played on artificial turf was Canada v USA on 24 September 1976 in Vancouver. The return game on 20 October 1976 at the Kingdome, Seattle, was the first World Cup match to be staged indoors.

LIMITED EDITION

On 1 June 1982 Nottingham Forest became a limited company after 117 years of being run by a committee with 209 club members.

DESIGNER KIT

On 26 January 1976 Kettering Town became the first English club to carry advertising on their shirts following a contract with a local tyre company. A month later the FA asked them to remove the sign. A compromise left them with the letter T.

BATMEN
East Stirling began life as a Falkirk cricket club called Bainsford Bluebonnets who changed their name to play football as Bainsford Britannia.

CORINTHIAN ORIGINS
Ipswich Town were members of the Amateur Football Alliance before turning professional in 1936. They played in the Southern Amateur League before joining the Eastern Counties League then the Southern League.

SOMEBODY IN THE CITY
The first club to play in the Football League with the name City were Lincoln in 1892. Stoke were one of the founder members of the Football League in 1888 but did not add City to their name until later.

JERSEY EXPORT
The first Channel Islander to become a Football League professional was Eric Hurel, an inside-forward who joined Everton from St Helier in April 1936.

LATICS SHORTS
Oldham Athletic's first game under their name was a friendly on 2 September 1899 against Berry's Reserves, a team of shoe blackers from Manchester. The game began half a hour late and Oldham began a man short, though he turned up later in a 1–0 win. At the end of the season, Oldham needed to beat Newton Heath Clarence to win the Manchester Alliance League, but fielded only seven players and lost 2–0 to finish third.

GUNNERS IN REVERSE ORDER

Throughout their history, Arsenal have had more than their share of players whose second names are quite common as first names. Using shirt numbers or positions here is a complete team down the years:

1. Dan LEWIS 1924–30
2. Laurie SCOTT 1946–51
3. Bob JOHN 1922–37
4. Trevor ROSS 1975–77
5. Ray DANIEL 1949–53
6. Michael THOMAS 1987–
7. Charlie GEORGE 1969–75
8. David JACK 1928–34
9. Mel CHARLES 1959–62
10. Alex JAMES 1929–37
11. Charlie NICHOLAS 1983–87

Manager: George GRAHAM 1986–

RELATIVELY SPEAKING

THE ALLEN CLAN
On 14 January 1989 Bradley Allen made his debut for Queen's Park Rangers against Wimbledon as substitute, to become the sixth member of the family to play in the Football League. The others were: father Les (Chelsea, Tottenham, QPR), uncle Dennis (Charlton, Reading, Bournemouth); brother Clive (QPR, Crystal Palace, Arsenal, Tottenham, Man City) and cousins Paul (West Ham, Tottenham) and Martin (QPR, West Ham).

FAMILY TIES
In 1991 the Linighan brothers Andy and David were joined as members of Football League clubs by their 17-year-old twin brothers Brian and John, trainees at Sheffield Wednesday. Andy with Arsenal was previously with Hartlepool United, Leeds United, Oldham Athletic and Norwich City while David at Ipswich was formerly with Hartlepool, Derby County and Shrewsbury Town. Eldest brother Mark, 30, was once on the books of Hartlepool but declined full-time terms and combines work as a fitter with playing for Bishop Auckland. Father Brian played for Lincoln and Darlington, his brother Michael for Middlesbrough.

FAMILY AFFAIR
On 17 October 1970 during the Leeds United v Manchester United Division One match, Leeds' Jack Charlton was booked then scored. United's Bobby Charlton scored his 199th first class goal for a club record in this 2–2 draw.

GEORGE THE SECOND
When Bill McCracken was Hull City's manager in the 1920s, he signed a goalkeeper called George Maddison. After the Second World War as Aldershot manager he signed his son George jnr as a goalkeeper.

FAMILY MATTERS
In the 1920s, Jimmy Nelson and Jimmy Blair were Scottish international full-back partners with Cardiff City. After the war, Blair's son was an inside-forward with Bournemouth and later Nelson's boy occupied a similar position at the same club.

In the 1930s Southampton had a goalkeeper called George Thompson and full-back called Charlie Sillett. In the 1950s George Thompson jnr was a Carlisle United goalkeeper, his brother Des kept goal for Sheffield United, while brothers Peter and John Sillett were Chelsea full-back sons of Charlie.

BROTHERLY CHANGE
Though Jimmy Mullen was a one-club man with Wolverhampton Wanderers and England, his brother Andy played for Aston Villa, Brighton & Hove Albion, Annfield Plain, Workington, South Shields and Scunthorpe United between 1948 and 1956.

GENERATION GAP
Jimmy Dunn (Everton) and Alec Herd (Manchester City) were on opposite sides in the 1933 FA Cup Final. Their sons were also at Wembley: Jimmy Dunn jnr (Wolverhampton Wanderers) in 1949 and David Herd (Manchester United) in 1963. On both occasions Leicester City were the opponents.

DOVE-TAYLORED
Yorkshire brothers Jack and Frank Taylor were not twins but they were full-back partners with Wolverhampton Wanderers before the Second World War and in June 1952 both became managers for the first time within a week of each other. During 1960–61 they both lost their jobs, Jack at Leeds, Frank at Stoke City.

FAMILY ENTERTAINMENT
Radnicki, a team from Pirot in Yugoslavia, were founded in 1921. For nearly 40 years they always had at least one member of the Zivkovic family in their team. One day they played against a complete team of Zivkovics. It was the first time they had not had one of them in their own side.

WIDESPREAD BENNETTS
Wally Bennett, an inside-left or centre-forward, who joined Barnsley in 1938 from Mexborough and later played for Doncaster Rovers and Halifax Town, was a member of a footballing family. His father, three uncles and a cousin all appeared in League football.

THE BUTLERS DID IT
During wartime regional football in 1916–17, Grimsby Town fielded Jack Butler, who had played for the club in the previous decade. In 20 games he played in eight of them with his son Bill as a colleague.

FAMILY AFFAIRS
Sheffield United's 1899 and 1902 FA Cup final teams included Harold Johnson, while sons Harold and Tom also played in the 1925 and 1936 finals for the club. The original teams also included Peter Boyle, whose son Tom played in the 1925 final.

PLENTY MO(O)RE
Right-winger Alan Moore was one of ten brothers, eight of whom were footballers. He also played for eight different clubs in his career between 1946 and 1959: Sunderland, Spennymoor, Chesterfield, Hull City, Nottingham Forest, Coventry City, Swindon Town and Rochdale.

BROTHERS OUT-OF-LAW
On 26 April 1986 Colchester United brothers Tom and Tony English were sent off along with Crewe Alexandra's Gary Blissett in a Division Four game. But Colchester won 2–0.

JACK'S THE BOYS
Plymouth Argyle manager Bob Jack sold three sons in turn to Bolton Wanderers: David, Robert and Rollo during the 1920s.

DOUBLE INDEMNITY
Exeter City defenders might have been forgiven for seeing double when Swindon Town beat them 2–0 in September

1946. The marksmen were the Stephens twins Alf and Bill, the first such pair to score in the same Football League game.

PRIORITIES RIGHT
In the summer of 1990 before John Major became Prime Minister, the family's holiday had to be postponed to allow his teenage son James to have a trial with Aston Villa. Major himself has been a lifelong Chelsea supporter.

OLD FATHER THAMES
In 1930–31 David Buchanan was the manager of Thames in Division Three (South) while his son Alec lead the attack from centre-forward.

PHIL FROM THE BLUES MAX
Phil Woosnam was capped by Wales while with West Ham United. His uncle Max had been a Manchester City amateur centre-half who played for England against Wales in 1922.

DATES ON THE CALLENDERS
The Callender brothers Tom and Jack played side by side in the half-back line for Gateshead in 46 League and 6 FA Cup games in 1952–53. Jack, a right-half, had joined the club in 1942; Tom, a centre-half, was signed three years later. He had previously played for Lincoln City making his debut in 1938–39. For Gateshead, Jack made 470 League appearances and scored 41 goals while Tom appeared 439 times and had 61 goals to his

'Blue is the colour . . .'

credit. They are one of only a few brothers in the game who have scored more than 100 goals between them as non-forwards. Tom, a penalty expert, scored 10 in one season (1949–50). In one period of eight years he missed only two League games.

An older brother, John, played for Walker Celtic, Chesterfield, Lincoln City, Port Vale and Gateshead!

MOTHERLY BACKGROUND

John Lumsden, a left-back with Aston Villa, Workington and Chesterfield in the 1960s, did not follow in his father's footsteps, but his mother had been a left-back with Smalley Ladies of Derbyshire.

DOUBLE HAT-TRICK

William Ewart Harrison managed to score one of Wolverhampton Wanderers' goals in their 3–1 FA Cup Final win against Sunderland in 1908. But his wife achieved her own hat-trick: presenting him with triplets on the same day.

NOBLE CAUSE

Paul Williams, the West Bromwich Albion forward signed from Stockport County in 1991, is the son of Betty Williams, who with Mairead Corrigan set up the Peace Movement in Northern Ireland and were awarded the Nobel Peace Prize.

DON'T JUST SAY BROWN

Eddy Brown was a Roman Catholic Teaching Brother until he decided against taking holy orders and went to work on the railway. He had jobs in the signal box, parcel office and as a ticket booking clerk before working nights in Preston station. Although he had played at school, it had never been for a team, but he asked Preston North End for a trial. The club sent trainer George Bargh to the station yard and for 20 minutes he had a kickabout with Brown. He was signed as an amateur in March 1948 at 22, scored four goals in an 'A' team game and 16 in seven matches before turning professional. He made his League debut in November 1950 against Sunderland at inside-right. Later he played for Southampton, Coventry City, Birmingham City and Leyton Orient scoring over 200 goals.

After leaving the league scene he was with Scarborough, Stourbridge, Bedworth Town and Wigan Athletic before retiring in 1964–65. Brown was a character who would often 'shake hands' with corner-flags after scoring a typically brilliant individual goal. He quoted Shakespeare in the dressing-room and off the field he modelled men's wear, refereed ladies soccer, lectured at prisons, judged beauty competitions and danced professionally for Geraldo and his Orchestra on television. He was also a fascinating after-dinner speaker. While player-manager of Scarborough he spent one Sunday looking for the gold tooth he had lost on the pitch the day before. It was his most unrewarding period on a football field as he did not find it.

AT HOME AND ABROAD

HONG KONG CHARLIE
Goalkeeper Charlie Wright's varied career, which began in the middle 1950s with Morton, progressed to Rangers, Workington, Grimsby Town, Charlton Athletic and Bolton Wanderers until 1971. Among three international appearances for Hong Kong while on National Service in the Lancashire Regiment, he played against Peru and saved a penalty in a 2–1 win.

GRASS ROOTS RECORD
Ipswich Town did not lose at home in the 1953–54 season until 23 January, some supporters putting their run of success down to a seven leaf clover given to them by a fan from America.

SCOTS ABSENT
Early in the 1990–91 season, Glasgow Rangers could have fielded an entire team without a Scot in it:
Chris Woods (England),
Gary Stevens (England),
Chris Vinnicombe (England),
Trevor Steven (England),
Terry Butcher (England),
Oleg Kuznetsov (USSR),
Pieter Huistra (Holland),
Terry Hurlock (England),
Mark Hateley (England),
Nigel Spackman (England),
Mark Walters (England).

CZAR'S IGNORED
Sweden played Russia twice before the First World War, in 1913 and 1914. Sweden won 4–1 in Moscow in the first game and drew 2–2 in Stockholm in the second. The Soviets do not acknowledge either match since it was under the Czar's regime.

THE WIGHT RESULT
The last time a club from off the mainland knocked a Football League side out of the FA Cup was when Newport (Isle of Wight) defeated Clapton Orient in 1945–46. Shrewsbury Town are the last Football League club to have played a tie there. They drew 0–0 with Newport in the first round in 1958–59.

DISPLACED PERSONS
During 1990–91 these Football League players might have been considered to be displaced persons: Neville Southall (Everton), Justin Edinburgh (Tottenham), Simon Charlton (Huddersfield), Trevor Putney (Middlesbrough), Andy Barnsley (Rotherham), Alan Devonshire (Watford), Kevin Kent (Mansfield), Andy Sussex (Crewe), Dion Dublin (Cambridge), Tim Sherwood (Norwich), Andy Hull (Leyton Orient). Substitutes: Derek Brazil (Oldham), Alan Paris (Notts County).

CHINESE CHECKER
On 15 May 1978, Jack Taylor, who had refereed the 1974 World Cup final, officiated at the Chinese Cup final between Tientsin and Hupeh Province.

ARGY BARGY

In the summer of 1953, the FA undertook a tour of South America. It began in Buenos Aires with an FA XI taking on an Argentine XI on 14 May, a match which is often either wrongly considered to have been a full international or totally ignored. The FA team: Ditchburn; Garrett, Eckersley, Wright, Barrass, Barlow, Berry, Bentley, Taylor, Redfern Froggatt, Jack Froggatt. The Argentines won 3–1.

Four days later in the full international against Argentina, heavy thunderstorms reduced the pitch to a farce and it was abandoned at 0–0 after only 21 minutes. This match *was* regarded as a full international!

CRAVEN COTTAGE PELE

Although Pele never played at Wembley, he did make one appearance in London as a player for his club Santos in a friendly at Fulham. He scored from a penalty but Fulham won 2–1 on 12 March 1973 in front of 21464.

SOVIET ORIGINS

Although Russian players in the Football League have become less rare in recent years, the nearest pre-war connection came from Jack Acquroff, a London born centre-forward, son of a Russian father. He played for Tottenham Hotspur, Hull City and Norwich City.

HOME AND AWAY
Terry Springthorpe, the former Wolverhampton Wanderers and Coventry City defender, emigrated to the USA to play for New York Americans, the oldest surviving professional team in the country, founded in 1931. He lived 200 miles from their ground and flew to home games. In 1956 the club, known as the Amerks, merged with Hakoah.

STOP OUT STEP IN
In 1956 Stop Out FC of New Zealand won the Chatham Cup in their Silver Jubilee Season.

TURKISH POT-POURRI
In 1990–91 Turkish football had foreigners from a variety of countries playing in their Division One, from Algeria, Argentina, Brazil, Britain, Germany, Poland, Romania, the USSR and Yugoslavia.

SWISS MISS
Arsenal's goalkeeper in a 3–2 win over Swiss Wanderers at Highbury on 21 September 1938 was George Swindin. When Arsenal had a tour of Europe in 1952 it included three games in Switzerland and Swindin was the only survivor from the original match.

CIAO ITALIA
In 1951–52 four British managers lost their jobs with Italian clubs: Frank Soo (Padova), Ted Crawford (Bologna), Denis Neville (Atalanta), and Jesse Carver (Juventus).

AYR GRADUATES
In 1989–90, four former Ayr

United players were enjoying success elsewhere: Alex Ferguson as manager of FA Cup winners Manchester United, Alan McInally winning a West German championship medal with Bayern Munich, Steve Nicol a League championship medal with Liverpool and Robert Connor with Skol Cup and Scottish Cup winners medals for Aberdeen.

HOTTE TROTTER
Bradford born Tim Hotte had two years as an apprentice with Arsenal but became homesick. He then had a trial with Bradford City but joined Huddersfield Town before drifting to Bradley Rangers, Harrogate Town for three years then Frickley Athletic. His next move was to accept an offer to play in Finland, but he was advised by the British Embassy not to go because two people had been taken hostage there. Halifax Town asked him to help them out only to find he had been classed as a Finnish citizen, even though he had never set foot in the country.

BELL WITH APPEAL
In October 1978 Willie Bell gave up his job as manager of Lincoln City to join a religious sect in America. He went there to coach the Campus Crusade for Christ team, hoping to convert sportsmen to christianity.

AWAY BUT AT HOME
In 1938–39 Sheffield United were showing fine away form in Division Two, but were dropping points at Bramall Lane chiefly in drawn games. For the last three home matches it was decided to treat them as away fixtures. Each morning of the

game the players assembled and were driven by bus to Derbyshire where they ate lunch and drove back to the ground. They picked up five points and secured promotion to Division One.

EAST MEETS WEST
Matthias Sammer, 23, became the first East German selected to play for the new united all-German team against Switzerland in Stuttgart on 19 December 1990. He began in the Dynamo Dresden Under-6 team and earlier in the season had joined Stuttgart for £730,000. Germany won 4–0. It was the first united team since 1942. When West Germany resumed internationals in 1950, their first match had been against Switzerland in Stuttgart on 22 November. They won 1–0.

Vorsprung Durch Technik . . . East German style

SCOTS TWO-TO-ONE
Of the three players who have each scored five goals in a League game for Cardiff City, only one is a Welshman: Walter Robbins. The other two were Hughie Ferguson and Jim Henderson, both Scots.

TRAVELLING MAN
Barnsley born Joe Hooley had played for seven clubs before his 21st birthday on Boxing Day 1959. Later he turned out for seven more before taking up coaching in Sudan, England, Iceland, Norway and Germany by 1977 when he was still only 38.

GOING, GOING BONG?
In 1955 Stoke City received a letter from a 21-year-old Russian outside-right Marcel Bong, who was living in Bremen, West Germany, offering himself for a trial.

FALKLANDS FACTOR
In April 1982 Stockport County considered changing their colours because they matched the Argentine national strip.

SHIP TO SHORE
Fred Davis (Wrexham) and Don Gibson (Sheffield Wednesday) were wing-halves. During the war they served together on the cruiser *Diadem*, often playing together in the ship's team.

STROLL ON
In November 1945 Queen's Park were grounded by fog after playing a friendly in Germany and their second team had to deputise for them in the fixture with Queen of the South. The Queen's Park Strollers lost 3–2.

NO CIAO SERVED
On 1 February 1971, the Italian players union complained that when Graziano Landoni refused to say goodbye to his trainer at Palermo, he was fined £670.

UNITED'S KINGDOM
In 1936–37 Manchester United had five professional goalkeepers all born in different countries: John Breedon and Leonard Langford (England), John Clunie (Scotland), Tommy Breen (Ireland) and Roy John (Wales).

GOALS AND GOALSCORING

NO PLACE LIKE HOME
Tottenham Hotspur forward Alan Gilzean did not score an away goal in the 1965–66 season among his 12 League goals. Eric Wildon's first 18 League goals for Hartlepool United in 1950–51 were scored at home, as were Wilf Grant's first 19 for Cardiff City the following season. Only one of Neville Coleman's 26 for Stoke City in 1956–57 was scored away.

TEN IN ROW CLUB
In 1961–62 Ron Rafferty (Grimsby Town) became the third player in the post-war period to have scored in every one of ten successive League games. The second had been Ralph Hunt in 1959–60, also for Grimsby, and both players had started their careers at Portsmouth. David Thomas (Plymouth Argyle) was the first in 1946–47.

STAMPING HIS AUTHORITY
Jack Stamps made his name with Derby County as a centre-forward, leading their attack in the 1946 FA Cup Final and scoring twice in their 4–1 win over Charlton Athletic. But his early career was anything but successful. He first played for Silverwood Colliery and joined Mansfield Town in October 1937, making his debut a month later at Reading on 13 November in a 3–2 defeat. At the end of the season he was given a free transfer and drifted to New Brighton in August 1938. After a dozen goals for the reserves in

as many games he was promoted to the first team because of injury to another player. He scored on his debut against Southport on 12 November 1938 but did not score again until he managed four goals in three games, though he had scored in an FA Cup tie. Derby moved in to sign him for £1500 in January 1939.

BLASTED HEATH
John Heath was not only the player who scored from the first penalty awarded in a first-class match in England, for Wolverhampton Wanderers against Accrington on 14 September 1891, he also scored a hat-trick for Arsenal in their first League win, against Walsall Town Swifts in a 4–0 win on 11 September 1893.

IN LIKE FLINT
Even as a ten-year-old, Ian Rush seemed destined to become a prolific goalscorer. Playing for St Mary's Primary School in Flint, he scored all eight goals in an 8–4 win one week and all six the next in a 6–4 success over the same opposition.

A ROVER'S RETURN
On 5 February 1955, Tommy Briggs scored seven goals in a row including one penalty for Blackburn Rovers in an 8–3 win over Bristol Rovers. Yet on 6 November 1954 he had failed to score in a 9–0 success over Middlesbrough.

NO OUTFIELD STRANGER

Ray Wood, the Manchester United goalkeeper in the 1957 FA Cup Final who bravely returned to play in the outfield after injury, had to wait a long time for a regular place. He even played at centre-forward in 'A' team games and once scored four goals.

OVER-30 CLUB

Not since 1935–36 when Raich Carter and Bob Gurney each hit 31 goals in Division One for Sunderland, has any club in the division had two players with 30 or more in a season's League football.

REAL MILESTONE

When Alfredo di Stefano reached 500 games for Real Madrid in September 1962 he had scored 424 goals. Of these 23 had come from penalty kicks, 22 from free-kicks. Of the other 379, 73 were headed goals. His best season was in 1956–57 when he scored 68 in 60 games. In those 500 matches he had been on the winning side 340 times and the losing side on 90 occasions.

ANY REVENGE IS BETTER

When Torquay United met Swindon Town on 8 March 1952 in Division Three (South), it was their fifth encounter that season. In the second round of the FA Cup the teams had drawn 3–3 and 1–1 before Swindon won the second replay 3–1. On 20 October 1951, Swindon had won their home match in the League 2–1. But in the return game at Torquay, United gained ample revenge winning 9–0. It was Torquay's highest win since they had entered the League. However they were helped by

injury to visiting goalkeeper Norman Uprichard who left the field after the fourth goal early in the second half.

SEVEN HERE HITCH

Don Robson had a midweek trial for Doncaster Rovers and scored seven goals. Signed on, he had difficulty in obtaining RAF leave and joined Gateshead in 1953. Bill Calder turned down offers of trials with Airdrie and Stirling Albion to go to Leicester City. Playing in a match for trialists only, he scored seven goals in a 9–1 win. Later he played for Bury and Oxford United.

STAN THE MAN

Stanley Matthews scored only one goal in the Football League during 1962–63. It was on 18 May in a 2–0 win over Luton Town at the Victoria Ground. It enabled Stoke to win the Division Two championship and relegated Luton.

DEAN'S MACHINE

On 7 February 1931, Everton won a Division Two game at Charlton Athletic 7–0. All five Everton forwards (Ted Critchley, Jimmy Dunn, Dixie Dean, Tom Johnson and Jimmy Stein) scored in a first-half spell of 17 minutes. Dean completed his hat-trick later.

TAYSIDE TRAUMA

On 21 February 1959, Dundee United were beaten 8–2 at Berwick Rangers in a Division Two match. Eric Addison scored six times for Berwick, a club record. In Division One, Dundee lost 6–4 at home to Motherwell for whom Gerry Baker scored four times.

IMMEDIATE RETURN

Tommy Spratt, 16, scored 14 goals on his debut in a 25–0 win for the Manchester United fifth team during 1957–58.

TOFFEES STUCK ON GOALS

Starting from 17 October 1931, Everton scored 33 goals in four consecutive home games: Sheffield Wednesday 9–3, Newcastle United 8–1, Chelsea 7–2 and Leicester City 9–2.

EIGHT TIMES FABLE

Jimmy Broad, the Millwall centre-forward in 1919–20, scored 32 goals while his nearest rival in the team managed only four.

EXECUTIVE CRECHE

Gordon Taylor, chief executive of the Professional Footballers Association, once scored 97 goals in a season as a schoolboy inside-forward. He graduated from Hurst Wesleyans to the Bolton 'B' side then the 'A' team, then made his reserve debut and his first team bow at 18.

ALLY HOISTS THE TOTAL

On 3 February 1990 Ally McCoist scored in a 3–1 win for Rangers over Dundee United in the Premier Division to become the club's leading post-war goalscorer. It was his 131st goal and he overtook Derek Johnstone's previous total.

WITHE OR WITHOUT

When Peter Withe was with Southport in 1971–72 as an amateur he was trying to regain full match fitness and turned out for Skelmersdale. Southport's manager Alex Parker took advantage of the rule allowing amateurs to play for more than one club providing they were in different leagues. Withe, who had been out of action for some time, scored in a 3–0 win and the following day played for Southport reserves.

STAGS IN UNISON

Ted Harston scored 11 hat-tricks for Mansfield Town in two seasons, 1935–36 and 1937–38. His first came on his debut against Southport in a 3–3 draw on 19 October 1935. These 11 trebles included one 7, two 5's and two 4's. He was top scorer in both seasons with 26 and 55 respectively. Curiously enough in each season Atkinson and Anderson, with 10 and eight goals respectively were second and third highest marksmen.

BYPASSING THE CLUTTERBUCK

During October and November 1898, Birmingham scored 35 goals without reply in four League and FA Cup games. They beat Chirk 8–0 in the cup, Luton Town 9–0 in the League and then Druids 10–0 in the cup before beating Darwen 8–0 in the League. Goalkeeper Jack Clutterbuck hardly touched the ball in six hours' play.

THE WALKDEN WONDER

Few players throughout history can claim to have scored as many as four goals on their debut in first-class football. Even rarer has been a quartet achieved at the expense of Liverpool.

Fred Howard was signed on 18 September 1912 by Manchester City from his local club Walkden Wednesday. He made his debut in Division One against Liverpool on 18 January 1913 and scored three times in the first 13 minutes. He went on to add a fourth in a 4–1 win. His career with City was interrupted by the First World War, but this centre-forward scored 43 League and Cup goals for them in 91 matches.

SIX OF THE BEST
On 13 February 1954, Everton beat Derby County 6–2 at the Baseball Ground. It was only the third time in their history that they had scored six times away from home in League games, all of them against Derby. In November 1882 Everton won 6–1 and in December 1890 it had been 6–2.

DOGGED AT DARLINGTON
Graham Doggart, who became chairman of the Football Association in the 1960s, assisted Darlington as an amateur during the 1921–22 season and scored five times in two League games.

LATE, LATE SHOW
On 28 November 1953 Crewe Alexandra were leading Stockport County 1–0 in a home Division Three (North) game with 30 minutes remaining. Stockport won 5–1, Jack Connor scoring a hat-trick. Connor later joined Crewe.

QUICK COLIN
On 8 December 1979, Colin Cowperthwaite of Barrow scored a goal in 3.58 seconds from the kick-off against Kettering Town. From the start of the game he received the ball and scored with his first touch. Barrow won 4–0 and Cowperthwaite scored four goals.

WILLIE'S FINAL STRIKE
In 1931–32 Motherwell forward Willie McFadyen overhauled the goalscoring record of Celtic's Jimmy McGrory with 52 goals in 38 Division One matches, achieving the feat in the last match of the season only minutes after missing a penalty.

FREEMAN'S FREE-FOR-ALL
During 1912–13 Burnley had a run of 10 Division Two wins. Leading scorer Bert Freeman scored 14 goals during these games ending with four in a 5–1 win over Leicester Fosse.

GAME OF TWO HALVES
On 4 March 1933 Coventry City led Queens Park Rangers 7–0 at half-time in a Division Three (South) game. But there was no further scoring in the second half.

ONE OVER THE EIGHT
On 2 November 1985 when Raith Rovers beat Stenhousemuir 9–2 it was a record score in the reorganised Division Two, formed in 1974. Keith Wright scored five goals including three in four minutes.

SIX OF ONE . . .
Davy Walsh scored in each of his first six Football League games for West Bromwich Albion in 1946–47. Charlie Wayman scored in his last six for Darlington in 1957–58.

STAN'S UNIQUE DOZEN
Stanley Mortensen scored in 12 consecutive FA Cup ties for Blackpool from 1945–46 to 1948–49 inclusive.

HENRY LXII

In 1947–48 Henry Morris scored 62 League and Cup goals for East Fife. In the League his scoring sequence was 1 1 1 2 2 1 2 2 1 1 1 2 2 3 4 2 1 2 2 3 2 2; the League Cup 2 2 2 1 3 1; the Scottish Cup 2 and the Supplementary Cup 3 4 1.

NINETY-MINUTE GAME

On 29 January 1977 at Ninian Park, Wrexham equalised at 2–2 against Cardiff City in the dying seconds of the game. There was just time for Cardiff to restart and score themselves through John Buchanan before the final whistle at 3–2 for City.

BLUNDER TO WONDERLAND

In 1976–77 Sunderland went 10 games without scoring a goal, then won the next four games, scoring 17 times.

FRIENDLY STAN

Stan Fazackerley once scored 11 goals for Hull City in a tour game in Norway against Trondheim & District on 28 May 1912 in a 16–1 win. He had scored one of the goals by which Hull had beaten Tottenham Hotspur in Brussels in the De Decker Cup on 12 May.

GOING THE WHOLE . . .

On 20 April 1910 James Hogg scored nine of the Hartlepools United goals in their 12–0 win over Workington in a North-Eastern League game.

TOP MAC

To find the highest goalscorer in Scottish League football in 1953–54 you had to look down at Division 'C' where John McCutcheon of Stranraer led with 39 goals.

SMOOTH CLYDESIDE

In 1952–53 right-winger John Buchanan scored in 11 successive Division One games for Clyde.

TOAST TO TEDDY

Teddy Sheringham's four goals for Millwall in the 4–1 win over Plymouth Argyle on 16 February 1991 marked several milestones. His first clocked up the 3200th Football League goal of the season, he overtook Derek Possee's club record of 79 League goals and he equalled John Calvey's 89 League and Cup goals achieved nearly a century earlier.

PAYNE RELIEF

Joe Payne's ten goals for Luton Town are renowned. The unrelated Brian Payne also scored ten goals for Huddersfield Town juniors against Doncaster Rovers juniors in January 1956 in the Northern Intermediate League. But he did not make his League debut until transferred to Gillingham.

EVANS THE BOOT

Bernard Evans scored after 25 seconds of his debut for Wrexham against Bradford City in September 1954.

POPPIES POPPED THEM IN

On Christmas Day 1935, Kettering Town won 9–1 away to Higham Town in the Northants League with Alex Linnell scoring four goals. On Boxing Day in the return game, Kettering won 20–3, Linnell adding seven to his holiday total. Then on 31 May 1947, in attempting to win the United Counties League on goal average, the Poppies beat Holbeach 18–0 with Arnold Woolhead creating an individual club record with 11 of the goals.

DAY TO REMEMBER
On 5 December 1970, the day Jimmy Greaves scored his 351st goal in 500 League games when West Ham United beat Derby County 4–2, George Best scored his 100th League goal for Manchester United in a 2–2 draw with Tottenham Hotspur.

CHELSEA MILESTONE
After Bob Whittingham scored

30 League goals for Chelsea in 1910–11, the individual club record lasted longer than any other in the Football League until it was overhauled by Jimmy Greaves with 32 in 1958–59.

WOLVES AND HORSES
Billy Hartill, who was Wolverhampton Wanderers centre-forward between 1928 and 1935, was appropriately nicknamed 'Hartillery' because he had previously served as a regular soldier in the Royal Horse Artillery. He still holds the Wolves scoring record of 164 League goals and twice hit five: on 12 October 1929 against Notts County and on 3 September 1934 against Aston Villa.

WHAT A COINCIDENCE

STEEL CITY VACANCIES

On 6 October 1975, Sheffield United dismissed manager Ken Furphy. Neighbours Sheffield Wednesday were managerless themselves at the time. Len Ashurst was appointed as Wednesday's manager on 15 October and the same day Jimmy Sirrel left Notts County to take over at Bramall Lane. Sirrel had no contract with Notts, but gave a month's notice saying that he could do both jobs for a few weeks.

LOW FIGURES

On 24 October 1990 Lincoln City's attendance of 1974 in Division Four against Rochdale was their lowest since returning to the League in August 1988. The same day Scarborough's 1329 in the game with Carlisle United was their lowest since being promoted to the League in 1987.

BOLTON TORIES

Pre-First World War Bolton Wanderers full-back Jack Slater later became Conservative MP for Eastbourne. Roy Hartle, a Bolton full-back in the 1950s and 1960s, was a Conservative Councillor for the local Halliwell Ward.

CREWE'S ADVANTAGE

Up to the end of the 1968–69 season, 17 players had been ordered off in games against Crewe Alexandra, more than any club in the country.

TWIST OF FATE

In a Division Three match between Mansfield Town and Bury on 5 February 1991 at Field Mill, Mansfield's goalkeeper Andy Beasley was sent off for a professional foul on Bury striker Tony Cunningham. Chris Withe, on loan to Mansfield from Bury, took over in goal and saved Cunningham's mishit penalty. Before the end of the game Mark Kearney, on loan to Bury from Mansfield, cleared the ball off the goal-line to enable Bury to win 1–0 from a ninth minute goal by Kevin Hulme.

DOUGAN REGIS

Centre-forward Derek Dougan who played for Distillery, Portsmouth, Blackburn Rovers, Aston Villa, Peterborough United, Leicester City, Wolverhampton Wanderers and Northern Ireland, had a coincidental link with royalty. His brother was married on the same day as Queen Elizabeth and Prince Phillip, another brother was born on the same day as Prince Charles, while Dougan himself became the father of a boy on the day after the Queen had her fourth child.

OWLISH APPEARANCE

Besides making his League debut against Sheffield Wednesday, Charlie Aitken, who made a record 561 League appearances for Aston Villa, also scored his first goal in March 1964 and celebrated his 200th appearance in August 1966 both against the Owls.

SEVEN ASIDES

From 1982 to 1989 Southend United won seven consecutive matches against Lincoln City, and the same number in successive games between 4 October 1924 and 6 December scoring 16 goals and conceding three. In the years between 1939 and 1983, Southend played Cardiff City seven times and lost each time. They also lost seven successive matches against Swindon Town between 1957 and 1960.

BURSTING WITH COINCIDENCE

On 4 November 1916, in a Midland section Principal Competition wartime regional league game at Anlaby Road between Hull City and Leeds City, the ball burst. Leeds' next visit was on 5 January 1918 and the ball burst again on almost the identical spot.

CHRISTMAS ODDITIES

On Christmas Day 1936, only one of 11 Division One games was not won by a home team. That was goalless draw between Charlton Athletic and Sunderland. On Boxing Day in the reverse set of fixtures there were eight home wins and three draws. On Christmas Day 1937 in Division Three (North) not a single team won on its own ground. Of nine completed games, four were drawn and five won by the away side. The other two were fog-affected fixtures:

Deflation strikes in the First World War

28

New Brighton v Oldham Athletic was abandoned at half-time at 0–0 while Port Vale v Lincoln City was postponed.

EXACT REVERSAL

In 1905 Aston Villa beat Newcastle United 2–0 in the FA Cup Final, in 1924 Newcastle beat Villa 2–0. In 1904 Manchester City beat Bolton Wanderers 1–0, in 1926 Bolton beat City 1–0 in that year's final. In 1922 Huddersfield Town beat Preston North End 1–0 in the final with a penalty winner, in 1938 Preston beat Huddersfield 1–0 with another spot kick.

NEAR TOTAL TYKES

In 1951–52, Rotherham United were the only club in the top two Divisions whose regular team were all Englishmen. In fact only one Rotherham player was not from Yorkshire, wing-half Colin Rawson born in Shirebrook, Nottingham.

ALL CHANGE FOR CREWE

On 30 November 1990 Cambridge United were beaten 4–3 at home by Crewe Alexandra. Cambridge did not lose another competitive match until 1 March following a club record run of 16 League and Cup games without defeat. They lost 3–1 at Crewe. In 1983–84 Cambridge had broken Crewe's 27-year-old record by registering their 31st successive game without a win.

VERSATILE DJ

In November 1971 Everton beat Liverpool 1–0, their scorer being David Johnson. By April 1978 Liverpool had stretched their unbeaten run against Everton to 15 games with a Johnson goal for the Reds.

RHYL PROBLEM

In 1956–57 Rhyl Athletic had three players called Denis Wilson and two who answered to the name of Billy Hughes.

THE HARRY LINE THEME

The name Harry Davis appeared in Sheffield Wednesday teams from 1892–93 to 1906–07. Smethwick born Harry Davis was signed from Birmingham St George in 1892 and played in the club's first ever Football League game. He left in 1899. Wednesday signed Wombwell born Harry Davis from Barnsley in January 1900 and he remained until 1907 when he retired with injury, becoming the team's assistant trainer.

PLYMOUTH SOUNDINGS

Vic Metcalfe played two successive League games for Hull City against Plymouth Argyle, on the first day of the 1958–59 season and the first of the 1959–60 season.

BIRTHDAY BOYS

In 1959–60 Aston Villa had two players on their groundstaff, John Sleeuwenhoek and Ralph Brown, born on the same day: 26 February 1944.

NEW YEAR DESOLATION

Three years in succession Paul Gascoigne had cause to rue the New Year. In 1989 he missed it because of injury, in 1990 he cracked his left arm and was absent for a month, then in 1991 he was sent off.

NICHOLLS AND TIMES

Ron Nicholls had an exacting baptism in senior football as goalkeeper for Bristol Rovers in 1955–56. On 31 December he made his League debut against Division Two leaders Sheffield Wednesday but finished on the winning side in a 4-2 scoreline. A week later he faced Manchester United, the Division One leaders, in the FA Cup third round but kept a clean sheet in a 4–0 win. Oddly enough in each game Rovers scorers were the same: Alf Biggs (2), Barrie Meyer and Geoff Bradford.

BROTHERLY DATES

Major Frank Buckley, former Wolverhampton Wanderers, Notts County, Leeds United and Walsall manager and his brother Chris, Aston Villa chairman, were born on the same day 9 November, three years between them.

LETTER CHANGE

Ian Lawson made his debut for Burnley in an FA Cup third round tie against Chesterfield in 1956–57 at the age of 17. He scored four goals and hit another hat-trick in the fourth round against New Brighton. Tommy Lawton had made his Burnley debut 21 years earlier at 16.

WRIST ACTION

Ray King made his debut in goal for Newcastle United in 1942 after several reserve games. At Everton he saved a Tommy Lawton penalty, punching the ball with both hands. He thought he had badly sprained both wrists but a later X-ray revealed that he had broken them. In the meanwhile he had played 15 games. He was not retained by Newcastle but subsequently had a trial with Leyton Orient at Northampton in a Division Three (South) game and broke one wrist again. Even when he drifted into local football he broke his jaw. But after a spell with Ashington, he was signed by Port Vale in May 1949 and made 252 League appearances and won England 'B' honours.

GEORGE STEWART CLAN

In the space of 18 months George Stewart, a centre-forward, moved from Accrington Stanley to Coventry City. In November 1958 goalkeeper George Stewart joined Bradford City from Stirling Albion and right-back George Stewart was tranferred to Barrow from Montrose.

TEN YEARS ON

The England team which played in the first schoolboy
international at Wembley and defeated Scotland 8–2 before a
crowd of 55000, was considered to be one of the finest ever to
represent their country at this level. Ten years after the event, the
eleven players had moved on to various careers inside and
outside the game, during the intervening time.

RON WARD . . . . Chesterfield, Arsenal trial;
(goalkeeper)   became bricklayer.

FRED COOPER . . . . West Ham United, then ran
(right back)   Stratford public house.

MALCOLM SPENCER . . . . . . Wolverhampton Wanderers
(left back, Captain)   ground-staff; metal worker
                                   and part-time player with
                                   Evesham United.

BRIAN TWAITES . . . . Crystal Palace and Arsenal
(right-half)   trials. Joined father's
                                   hairdressing business; ran his
                                   own salon in Tunbridge Wells.

RON COPE . . . . Manchester United
(centre-half)

EDDIE CLAMP . . . . Wolverhampton Wanderers,
(left-half)   England full international.

MICHAEL CHARLTON . . . . . Chelsea, England youth
(right wing)   international. Motorcycle
                                   accident ended career.
                                   Salesman in cosmetics firm.

JOHNNY HAYNES . . . . Fulham, England youth, Under-23,
(inside-right)   full England international.

GEORGE BROWN . . . . Liverpool, Chesterfield,
(centre-forward)   Peterborough United then
                                   dropped out of game.

RAY PARRY . . . . Bolton Wanderers, Blackpool,
(inside-left)   England Under-23, full
                                   international.

JIM SCOTT . . . . Burnley
(left wing)

REPEAT
PERFORMANCES

LIFE AFTER MANAGER
In 1969–70 Forfar Athletic parted company with manager Jake Young. He turned out in a trial match for Arbroath reserves and was immediately signed by them as a player.

In 1987–88 injury appeared to have brought Jim Duffy's career to an end at Dundee. The following season he became Falkirk manager. But he resigned and against medical advice, resumed his playing career first with Dundee and then at Partick Thistle.

COINCIDENTAL EVENTS
New Brighton won their first four Division Three (North) games of the 1950–51 season: 2–0, 1–0, 1–0 and 1–0 before losing 4–0 away to Gateshead. They did not win again until 2 December when remarkably they won 2–0, 1–0, 1–0 and 1–0 followed by a 4–0 defeat at Stockport County. They then completed 17 games without a win taking two points and scoring only six goals, three of them in one game. At the end of the season New Brighton had scored 40 goals. Their top scorer was Jackie Jones with seven. In the club's first League season in 1923–24, 40 goals had also been their total with Billy Crooks top scorer with seven. At the end of the 1950–51 season they were not re-elected.

VINNY REGRET
On 19 January 1991 in a Division One match at Maine Road, Sheffield United's Vinny Jones was booked after five seconds

for a foul on Manchester City player-manager Peter Reid. After 55 minutes he was booked again for another foul on the same player and sent off. Manchester City won 2–0.

WOOD FATIGUE
On 22 August 1970 there was a 45 minute delay during the match between Lincoln City and Brentford when a goalpost broke. After being repaired the outstanding three and half minutes of play were completed. The following week another goalpost broke during the Swindon Town v Sunderland match.

LUCAS TREBLE
In November 1970 Billy Lucas returned as manager of Newport County for a Football League record third time.

DUAL CONTROL
David Steele left Bradford Park Avenue to become Huddersfield Town manager in September 1943, but also remained in charge of the Bradford club until a new manager was appointed.

PALACE OF VARIETIES
Peter Simpson not only scored a hat-trick on his debut for Crystal Palace in September 1929 but during the following season scored a total of ten League and Cup hat-tricks including one 6 and two 4's.

The three card trick?

FAMOUS FIRSTS
John Reid Smith was the first Scot to score at Wembley and the first to win and score in Cup finals at both Hampden Park and Wembley. He had scored Kilmarnock's winning goal in the 1920 Scottish Cup final and registered Bolton Wanderers second goal in the 1923 FA Cup final.

CLYDE GLIDE
On 31 October 1896, Clyde beat Woolwich Arsenal 3–2 at Plumstead in a friendly. The two teams met again in a floodlit match at Highbury on 20 September 1955. Clyde won again, 2–1.

HOT-STUFFED
During the 1990–91 season, Nigel Pepper of York City was sent off three times against Darlington; twice in Division Four games and once in an FA Cup tie.

PROFIT AND LOSS
Raich Carter, inside-forward with Sunderland in 1937 and Derby County in 1946 was the only player who appeared in an FA Cup winning team before and after the Second World War. Willie Fagan, inside-forward with Preston North End in 1937 and Liverpool in 1950 was the only one to figure in beaten Cup Finals over the same period.

THE DOUGHTY DOZEN
In 12 seasons with Blackpool, goalkeeper George Farm did not miss an FA Cup tie. Including three finals he played in 47 games.

CLASS OF '66
On 28 July 1985 in a match played at Leeds for the victims of the Bradford City fire disaster, the 1966 England World Cup team beat their West German counterparts 6–4. Geoff Hurst, at 46 years of age, repeated his hat-trick achievement of 19 years earlier.

DOUBLE BILL
Bill Lambton was trainer and manager to two Football League clubs in turn during 1958–59. He began as Leeds United trainer, was appointed manager in December and resigned in March to become Scunthorpe trainer-coach. In April he became their manager.

CHARLES THE THIRD
Charles Davis, a centre-half, was with Torquay United when they entered the Football League in 1927, at York City similarly in 1929 and again with Mansfield Town when they made their bow in 1931.

MATURE WOOD
Goalkeeper Alf Wood is not only the oldest player to have made a first team appearance for Northampton, at 39 years 351 days against Walsall on 30 April 1955, but he achieved a similar milestone with Coventry City, at 44 years 207 days against Plymouth Argyle in an FA Cup second round tie on 7 December 1958.

YO-YO EXPERT
Redfern Froggatt was in three Sheffield Wednesday teams which were relegated from Division One to Two in 1951, 1955 and 1958, and a member of four promoted sides in 1950, 1952, 1956 and 1959 when he captained them.

NEIGHBOURS
Goalkeeper Bob Anderson helped both Bristol Rovers and Bristol City to promotion from Division Three (South) in the 1950s. Billy Meredith and Sandy Turnbull played for Manchester City when they won the FA Cup in 1903–04. Five years later they teamed up again for Manchester United when they won the same trophy.

LONG SHOTS FOR CUP
In January 1953, Blackpool's Tom Garrett scored an FA Cup tie goal against Huddersfield Town from 56 yards and on the same day Queen's Park Rangers Tony Ingham scored another from 65 yards against Gillingham.

A DIFFERENT
BALL GAME

ALL-ROUND SWINGERS
On 7 April 1939, during the Easter weekend, Dixie Dean and Alex James showed their prowess at golf. Dean, then with Sligo Rovers, won both his matches in the opening rounds of the West of Ireland championships and James won the bogey competition at his South Herts club.

A BOBBY DAZZLER
While undergoing his National Service, Bobby Charlton won the high jump, javelin and 880 yards at an Army sports day.

EARLY RISER
When David Oliphant turned professional with Wolverhampton Wanderers at 17 in June 1959 he was already an all-rounder. He had been an England rugby school trialist and was an expert swimmer, diver, miler, sprinter, cricketer and cross-country champion.

SQUARING UP
In 1972–73 Bobby Thomas, a boxing manager, offered a new career to Roger Davies the Derby County centre-forward, as a heavyweight.

Bobby Charlton, footballer supreme and an all-round athlete in khaki

NETTING ALL-ROUND

Gordon Bradley, the Scunthorpe United, Leicester City and Notts County goalkeeper, was something of a penalty taker himself and combined football with being a professional tennis player.

BOXING NOT CLEVER

Doug Fletcher was ABA lightweight boxing champion but also keen to pursue a footballing career with Sheffield Wednesday. However the rules of boxing were such that he could not follow an amateur career and play professional football. He decided on the ball game and subsequently played for Bury, Scunthorpe United, Darlington and Halifax Town, John Charles had a similar problem and chose soccer.

FORD ANGULAR

On 28 November 1981 Stoke City gave a first team debut to Steve Ford, signed from Lewes and a former National League basketball player, away at Wolverhampton Wanderers. Stoke lost 2–0.

TIMELY
APPEARANCES

CHARLIE OVERSHADOWED
Charlie Buchan's lengthy and
distinguished first-class career
came to an end on 5 May 1928.
His last game was against
Everton at Highbury. The match
ended in a 3–3 draw, but the
event was overshadowed by
Dixie Dean scoring his record
60th League goal of the season.

BAKER'S DOZEN – LESS TWO?
Alf 'Doughy' Baker is the only
Arsenal player to have appeared
in every position on the field,
including goal, in first team
games. Chiefly a right-half, he
made 403 League and Cup
appearances, scoring 40 goals
between 1919 and 1930. He was
capped by England on one
occasion. Arsenal manager Leslie
Knighton signed him at the
pithead at Ilkeston to thwart
other interested parties.

**BILLY THE KIDD – A PETER
PAN**
Billy Kidd, a left-back, was given
a month's trial by Chesterfield
from his home town club
Pegswood United in 1931. He
was turned down but
subsequently recalled and
signed for them. He became a
regular choice and added to his
appearances when duties
permitted during the Second
World War. Despite being in his
late thirties he was still a first
team selection when normal
League football resumed in
1946–47 and made his last senior
appearance on 20 September
1947 at the age of 40 years 232
days.

BIG IMPRESSION
Ian Little signed for
Meadowbank Thistle on 25
August 1990 at the age of 16
years 8 months. He made his
debut as a substitute against
Clyde on 22 September and
scored his first goal the
following week against
Clydebank, again after coming
on as a replacement. He then
scored in the next three games.

BOURNE FREE
On 27 November 1974, Derby
County were playing Velez
Mostar in the UEFA Cup third
round first leg game at the
Baseball Ground and losing 1–0.
Manager Dave Mackay sent on
both substitutes: Jeff Bourne
scored twice and Alan Hinton
once to give Derby a 3–1 win.

MODEST CELEBRATIONS
On 7 September 1985, Arbroath
celebrated the Centenary of their
36–0 Scottish Cup win over Bon
Accord with a 1–1 draw at
Stenhousemuir, but the result
kept them at the top of Division
Two.

SWAN-UPPING (1)
On 12 March 1991 Southend
United travelled to Swansea City
for a Division Three match
having not won there in 17
attempts since 1920 when both
entered the League. Swansea
scored first but Southend won
4–1 to inflict on the Welsh club
their record seventh successive
defeat.

A SEMPLE STORY

In 1913 Billy Semple was outside-right in Southport's team beaten in the FA Cup by Carlisle United in a fourth round qualifying tie. Later he was appointed Southport's player-coach to the reserves, became groundsman, assistant trainer, eventually head trainer and then groundsman again. While he was still there Southport beat Carlisle 1–0 in the 1953–54 FA Cup first round proper.

LUCKY BLACK CAT

Shortly after the Second World War a small black cat with an injured tail came into the Stoke City club offices. 'Blackie' had arrived at a bad time in the team's fortunes. Bandaged, given full board and lodging, a bed in the referee's room and a seat in the stand on match days he stayed to see improved performances on the field.

REUNIONS

Several neighbouring post-war managers had been playing colleagues in earlier times. Bert Tann (Bristol Rovers) and Fred Ford (Bristol City) were contemporary Charlton Athletic centre-halves in the 1930s, Andy Beattie (Nottingham Forest) and Frank Hill (Notts County) were at Preston North End at the start of the Second World War, and Harry Potts (Burnley) and Jack Marshall (Blackburn Rovers) were together on Burnley's groundstaff at the same time.

NEAR DOUBLE CENTURIAN

Ernie 'Tug' Wilson, signed by Brighton & Hove Albion from Denaby United in 1922, played 14 consecutive seasons and made 558 League and Cup appearances, his 509 in the League alone being a club record. He tried on two occasions to make 100

The Victoria Ground Executive Cattery

appearances in succession but was deprived both times by injury on 99.

FIVE YEAR DELAY
Arthur Turner can claim to have played in an FA Cup Final but then had to wait five years before his League debut. He played in the 1946 Final for Charlton Athletic as an amateur but subsequently signed professional forms for Colchester United, then outside the League. He had to wait until the 1950–51 season when Colchester were elected to Division Three (South) for his baptism in the Football League.

OVER-THE-HILL MAN
Jack Hillman, the Burnley goalkeeper between 1891–92 and 1901–02, making 175 League appearances, turned out for the club during the First World War Regional League games at the age of 47 in 1917–18.

TIME WARP
In a Group Three match between Brazil and Sweden during the 1978 World Cup finals in Argentina, the South Americans were awarded a corner. Referee Clive Thomas allowed the kick to be taken although it was timed electronically at three seconds over the normal 90 minutes. Zico headed in with nine seconds of injury time on the clock but the goal was ruled out as the official insisted he had ended the match when the corner was taken.

Thomas had once added three-quarters of an hour to normal playing time for stoppages. It was a Boys Club match on the top of a mountain at Blaengwynfi and every time

the ball went out of play it rolled down the mountainside. The game lasted two and a quarter hours.

BLICK OF AN EYELID
Mickey Blick went from playing third team soccer to a European match in 10 days. The Swindon Town defender was called in at the last minute for injured centre-half Frank Burrows in the second leg of the Anglo-Italian League Cup Winners Cup match against Roma during 1969–70.

HARPER'S BIZARRE
Plymouth Argyle caused a few eyebrows to be raised when they played their head trainer Bill Harper in goal against Sheffield Wednesday. It was his first game for three years. The match ended in a 1–1 draw.

ABLE ABEL
On 9 March 1991 Atletico Madrid goalkeeper Abel Resino established a world record of 1230 minutes without conceding a goal, following the team's 3–0 win against Osasuna in Pamplona. Abel, 31, passed the 1143 minutes achieved by Dino Zoff in the Italian national team from 1972–74. His unbeaten run also overhauled the previous Spanish domestic record of 1223 established in 1988–89 by Manolo Lopez of the Division Two club Ceuta. Abel eventually took his unbeaten run to 1275 minutes.

HIRING A COACH
On 21 November 1981, Huddersfield Town were forced to include Steve Smith in their FA Cup first round tie at Workington because of injuries

and suspensions. He was coach to the juniors and had not played for four years. The game ended 1–1.

PREMATURE ANNOUNCEMENT
On 14 May 1976 Peter Shilton, with 21 caps for England, pulled out of the squad and asked not to be considered for selection in future. He had been kept out of the side by Ray Clemence. On 26 August he asked to be reconsidered and went on to win 125 caps.

BETTER LATE . . .
The oldest player to appear in a first class game for Fulham was Scottish international Jimmy Sharp, a full-back during his career. At the age of 40 he was called upon to play inside–left against Bury at Gigg Lane on 17 April 1920. The regular inside-forward Harold Crockford had missed the bus to the game. Sharp, the Fulham trainer, had retired as a player pre-war, but he managed to score what proved to be the only goal he ever managed in League football in a 2–2 draw.

NOT A PERENNIAL
Arthur Perry was a left-back who signed for Hull City in February 1947. He spent nine years there without a first team appearance. In July 1956 he was transferred to Bradford Park Avenue and established an immediate first team place.

WEARING OF THE GREEN
On 22 December 1990 during the Division Three match between Huddersfield Town and Bury, Huddersfield goalkeeper

Lee Martin was sent off for a professional foul in the 57th minute when Bury were leading 1–0. Kieran O'Regan took over the green jersey but was called upon to take a penalty in the 71st minute which put the teams level at 1–1. Huddersfield won 2–1. Eight minutes before the end of the game Bury's Ronnie Mauge was also sent off.

LATE CLOCKING ON
Brian Hornsby, Arsenal's substitute, came on against Manchester United on 25 August 1973 with only three seconds of the match remaining. Arsenal won 3-0.

ONE TOUCH FOOTBALL
On 15 September 1990 Andy Rammell, Barnsley's £100000 signing from Manchester United, made his debut as substitute at Blackburn Rovers in Division Two. He came on in the 81st minute but had to wait five minutes before he made his first contact with the ball. When he did, he scored the winning goal with a header in a 2–1 win.

A WEMBLEY FAREWELL
Joe Hulme's illustrious career as a right winger for Arsenal and Huddersfield Town ended when he announced that the FA Cup Final for Huddersfield against Preston North End on 30 April 1938 at Wembley was to be his last first-class game.

WELL-WORN WARNES
On 17 February 1951, Aldershot were at home to Nottingham Forest in a Division Three (South) game. Ten minutes before half-time their goalkeeper George Warnes was carried off

with a head injury and within seconds of returning he sustained damage to his right knee and had to be stretchered off. He began the second half bandaged from ankle to thigh, but played heroically with his concerned manager crouched on one side of the goal and the trainer on the other. Warnes made a billiant save in the dying seconds to enable his team to win 1–0 and he was carried off the field shoulder high by two Forest players, Wally Ardron and Colin Collindridge, who had been colleagues of Warnes earlier at Rotherham United.

'I can cope OK, but will somebody please scratch my nose?'

ALL IN TENS

The fastest goal recorded by a Huddersfield Town player was by Ken Willingham after 10 seconds in a Division One match against Sunderland on 14 December 1935. It was the only goal of the game. In December 1945 Willingham was transferred to Sunderland for £5000.

RAMSEY'S WATERHOLE

In December 1973 a Tunbridge Wells property developer opened a new public house and named it after Sir Alf Ramsey, who attended the opening and pulled the first pint. In May 1974 Ramsey was sacked as England manager.

LENGTHY KNEE-JERK REACTION

Justin 'Jack' Kneeshaw made his debut for Bradford City on 8 February 1908 against Wolverhampton Wanderers. His next came on 28 August 1920 for Cardiff City against Stockport County. But in the intervening years he had played for Cardiff in the Southern League.

JIM'S IN

On 15 December 1990 Jim Gallacher, the 39-year-old Clydebank goalkeeper, equalled Sandy Jardine's Scottish League record in his 634th appearance in a 1–1 draw with Raith Rovers.

FOOTBALL AND FISHING

Over the last 60 years the Football League can claim to have produced a team with definite 'fishy' connections.

MIKE SALMON . . . . Blackburn Rovers, Stockport County

RAY WHALE . . . . West Bromwich Albion, Southend United

PETER HADDOCK . . . . Newcastle United, Leeds United

LEN ROE . . . . Brentford

KEN FISH . . . . Aston Villa, Port Vale

JOHN SCALES . . . . Leeds United, Bristol Rovers, Wimbledon

RAY GILL . . . . Manchester City, Chester City

TOMMY SPRATT . . . . Manchester United, Bradford PA, Torquay United, Workington, York City, Stockport County

ANDY FLOUNDERS . . . . Hull City, Scunthorpe United

CHRIS PIKE . . . . Fulham, Cardiff City

HARRY HERRING . . . . Hartlepool United

42

HAZARDOUS
JOURNEYS

JOE WITH LATE WHEELS
The last Tottenham Hotspur first team squad member to acquire a car in August 1967 was Joe Kinnear. He bought a Corsair Automatic and travelled daily from his Watford home to White Hart Lane.

EXCURSION TRIP
The longest journey involving non-league teams in the FA Cup was Folkestone's visit to Stockton in 1951–52.

OVERNIGHT LAP
On 29 December 1990, Swansea City had decided to stay overnight near Wigan to avoid travelling on the day of the Division Three match. Unfortunately they were held up in traffic on the way to the ground and arrived late. But they did manage to win 4–2.

HILL'S DEBUT
Frank Hill's first appearance for Aberdeen nearly did not happen after he was selected to play for them at Paisley against St Mirren on 1 September 1928. The team travelled from Aberdeen on Friday and Hill arranged to join the party at Forfar. But he found a friend going to Glasgow and when the train arrived he was given permission to travel with him. Hill was to join the rest of the team in Glasgow. But on arrival he found everyone had left the station and he had no idea which hotel they had booked into. Another friend put him up at Stirling and he arrived at the ground at the crack of dawn expecting to be dropped. But everything was smoothed over. Alas there was no happy ending, St Mirren won 5–2.

MINE'S A DOUBLE
Billy Meredith's debut for Manchester City at Newcastle United on 27 October 1894 came in the middle of a hectic weekend for him. He worked in the pit on Friday and took the train at 2 o'clock Saturday morning, travelling until 11 o'clock. After the match he set off for home again reaching there at half past ten on Sunday morning. The same night he went back to work at the mine. City had lost the game 5–4.

GROUNDS TO FORGET
Bradford was not the favourite venue for Aldershot full-back Tony Devereux. He was sent off at Valley Parade against Bradford City in March 1962 and at Park Avenue against Bradford in February 1964. For Halifax full-back Walter Bingley, it was Newport which provided him with two dismissals.

TRAVEL WEARY
On the last Saturday in January 1937 there were 35 Football League and FA Cup games played and not one produced an away win.

SNOW ENTERTAINMENT

On 15 March 1947, when Third Lanark were using Hampden Park as a temporary home ground, their opponents Kilmarnock arrived more than an hour late because of travelling difficulties caused by snow. To keep the crowd amused a scratch game of Third Lanark reserves and Queen's Park played a seven-a-side game. Kilmarnock eventually won the delayed match 4–1.

DODGIN CARS

On 31 October 1970, Fulham manager Bill Dodgin jnr had to take a taxi the last 20 miles to Torquay to hand in the team names in time. Bristol Rovers manager Bill Dodgin snr had a similar deadline to meet at Rotherham and after a breathless run, managed to grab a lift with a motorist to the ground.

WAR WITHDRAWALS

During the Second World War, Dundee declined to participate in the North-Eastern League and as a consequence were out of senior football between June 1940 and August 1944. But during the First World War when they wanted to carry on, they were asked to withdraw from Division One for 1917–18 and 1918–19 to ease travelling for West of Scotland clubs. Division two had already been put in abeyance for the duration.

Hitch-hikers guide to the gallop-see?

GEOGRAPHICAL NIGHTMARE

During 1907–08 when the Southern League was anxious to keep up its numbers because of losses to the Football League, they included Bradford Park Avenue among their teams. Their 'local derby' was against Northampton, 130 miles away.

PULLING POWER

In December 1990, Wolverhampton Wanderers goalkeeper Mike Stowell hired a tractor to beat the snow storms of the West Midlands in order to report for his first international duty in Algeria for the England B team.

SPECTATOR SEES MOST OF THE ACTION

Of countless charity games played during the Second World War, one of the most outstanding took place at Anfield on 19 April 1941 for the Lord Mayor of Liverpool's War Fund. A Football League XI played an All-British XI. It produced 16 goals. The teams were:

Football League: Hobson (Chester); Lambert (Liverpool), Gorman (Sunderland), Willingham (Huddersfield), Pryde (Blackburn), Galley (Wolves), Worrall (Portsmouth), Dorsett (Wolves), Lawton (Everton), Stephenson (Leeds), Hanson (Chelsea).

All-British XI: Poland (Liverpool); Cook (Everton), Jones (Blackpool), Dearson (Birmingham), Cullis (Wolves), Busby (Liverpool), Nieuwenhuys (Liverpool), Mutch (Preston), Fagan (Liverpool), Stevenson (Everton), McShane (Blackburn).

Frank Swift who should have been in goal for the League was unable to play and his place was taken by Alf Hobson. He had the misfortune to be injured in a clash with Willie Fagan and so Billy Liddell, not long after his 19th birthday, was given his first taste of representative football as substitute. Tom Galley took over in goal with Liddell the outfield replacement.

The scoring went like this:

Stephenson 1–0, Nieuwenhuys 1–1, Dorsett 2–1, Cullis 2–2, Lawton 3–2, Busby 3–3, Lawton 4–3, Liddell 5–3, Fagan 5–4, Fagan 5–5, Hanson 6–5, Lawton 7–5, Stephenson own goal 7–6, Dorsett 8–6, Stevenson 8–7, Hanson 9–7.

Harry McShane's son is Ian McShane of *Lovejoy* fame.

EVENTFUL
CUP TIES

ONE TOUCH GOAL
On 10 January 1989 Watford scored with their first touch of the ball in an FA Cup Third Round replay at home to Newcastle United. Newcastle kicked off, and kept possession through the first minute until goalkeeper Dave Beasant was penalised for carrying the ball outside the penalty area. From Watford's free-kick, Neil Redfearn scored.

LUCKY ARSENAL
In Arsenal's first season in the FA Cup, 1889–90, they met Thorpe (Norfolk) in a second qualifying round tie away and drew 2–2 after extra time. Thorpe players were unable to travel for the replay and Arsenal were given a walkover.

LUCK OF THE DRAW
The third round draw of the FA Cup on 11 January 1947 had ten London clubs engaged: Brentford, Charlton Athletic, Chelsea, Fulham, Millwall, Queen's Park Rangers, Tottenham Hotspur and West Ham United were all at home; Arsenal were at Chelsea and only Crystal Palace were playing outside the area, at Newcastle United.

BRIGHTON CLANGER
On 28 November 1973, Clive Foskett of Walton & Hersham scored a hat-trick in eight minutes, late in the second half, as his team beat Brighton & Hove Albion 4–0 in an FA Cup first round replay. Brian Clough was Brighton's manager at the time.

DECOY DECEPTION
In an FA Cup fourth round tie between Liverpool and Wolverhampton Wanderers at Anfield on 2 February 1952 the normal acceptance of shirt numbers referring to playing positions was cunningly ignored by Liverpool. Wolves had put Billy Wright at right-half to keep a close watch on Billy Liddell, the Liverpool left-winger. But at the kick-off Liddell switched to centre-forward and Cyril Done appeared on the wing. It was ten minutes before Wolves sorted themselves out, by which time they were 2–0 down. Liverpool eventually won 2–1 with goals from Bob Paisley and Done.

BARNET FAIR FIRE
On 31 January 1959 in a second round Amateur Cup tie between Barnet and Willington, three goals were scored in 75 seconds. Barnet, who scored two of these, won 8–4.

(GRIM)SBY START
Grimsby Town's first experience in the FA Cup in 1882–83 was not a pleasant one. In the first round their Scottish opponents Queen's Park refused to travel and withdrew. On 25 November in the second round they entertained Phoenix Bessemer, a Rotherham works side. Phoenix won 9–1.

SIMPLY ALL ROSS

On 28 January 1991 in a Scottish Cup second round replay at Queen of the South's Palmerston Park, Highland League opposition Ross County were without their regular goalkeeper Mike Ure, who had been unable to obtain time off from work. His replacement Ross Cathcart turned his ankle badly during the pre-match warm-up, but bravely carried on and Ross County pulled off a shock 6–2 win over their Division Two rivals.

MANAGERS UNITE

On 5 November 1990 in a Leyland Daf Cup preliminary round game between Halifax Town and Rotherham United, visiting manager Billy McEwan stood with visiting fans after being sent off from the dugout in the 77th minute. Halifax manager Jim McCalliog left his place in the dugout in protest at the decision.

BAR TO SUCCESS

On 13 January 1923, Tottenham Hotspur met Worksop Town of the Midland League in the first round of the FA Cup. Worksop had surrendered their home draw and played away at White Hart Lane. With four minutes of the match remaining, Worksop hit the crossbar but the ball was scrambled clear. Spurs won the replay 9–0.

BRIGHTON PEERLESS

Few clubs can claim to have reached the fifth round of the FA Cup and ended their involvement in the competition having scored 43 goals. But it happened to Brighton & Hove Albion in 1932–33. After failing to apply for exemption they had

Exit left, one manager to cries of 'Off, Off!'

to play through from the qualifying rounds beating Shoreham 12–0, Worthing 7–1, Hastings 9–0, Barnet 4–0, Crystal Palace 2–1, Wrexham 3–2 after a 0–0 draw, and then met Chelsea. From the kick-off Brighton's Potter Smith sent Tug Wilson away but Len Allum checked the movement for Chelsea. The ball broke to David Walker who found Arthur Attwood with a brilliant through ball. With two opponents in pursuit, Attwood swerved to the right and hit the ball past Vic Woodley in the Chelsea goal, scoring inside 30 seconds. Brighton won 2–1 and then beat Bradford Park Avenue 2–1 in the fourth round. But West Ham held them to a 2–2 draw and Albion then lost 1–0 in the replay after extra time.

OVERTIME BAN
In the 1879–80 FA Cup first round Nottingham Forest and Sheffield drew 2–2, but Sheffield were disqualified for refusing to play extra time.

UNFORGETTABLE EXPERIENCE
After a 0–0 draw with Airdrie at Easter Road in the War Cup semi-final on 13 April 1940, Dundee United faced the replay four days later knowing that their opponents were to field Stanley Matthews as a guest player on the right wing. It was a daunting prospect for United's virtually unknown teenage full-back Tommy Dunsmore. But the youngster acquitted himself well and had the extra satisfaction of scoring United's third goal from the penalty spot in a 3–1 win.

A CLOSE CALL
On 22 September 1970 in a League Cup replay at Anfield,

Liverpool beat Mansfield Town of Division Three 3–2 after a goalless draw at Mansfield. Liverpool were trailing 2–1 with nine minutes remaining. Then they were awarded a controversial penalty for hands from which they equalised to force extra time, during which they scored the winning goal.

INTOXICATING DELAY
On the way to winning the FA Cup in 1932, Newcastle United were held to a 1–1 draw at home to Division Three (North) side Southport. The replay was also drawn 1–1 but in the second replay United won 9–0.

CUP BLUES
Coventry City's early association with the FA Cup was very much hit or miss. In 1900–01 they withdrew against Oswestry Town to fulfill a League fixture and might have been better advised to find a similar excuse the following season. They lost 11–2 away to Berwick Rangers and one of their goals was even scored by an opponent.

HAULED OVER THE GOALS
When Preston North End beat Hyde 26–0 in the FA Cup on 15 October 1887 they scored only four times in the first half-hour. But after that they speeded up with six in seven minutes. The referee allowed eight minutes overtime and during this they scored goal number 26.

LETTING DOWN LIGHTLY
A week after beating Darwen 11–1 in the FA Cup, having been 8–0 ahead at half-time, the Arsenal programme notes for the game versus Birmingham on

16 January 1932 read: 'Darwen may at first shock have felt humiliated by the magnitude of their defeat, but they could not fail to appreciate that it would have been a slight had we acted otherwise than we did.'

STAG AT BAY

Chris Staniforth had four spells with Manchester Town. Originally with Creswell Colliery, he joined Mansfield in 1921 from Chesterfield. He left for Oldham Athletic, returning in 1924. Notts County was his next stop but he came back to the Stags in 1926 only to leave after a season to go back to Notts County. In 1928 he began his fourth stint at Mansfield.

On 26 January 1929 Mansfield played Arsenal at Highbury in a fourth round FA Cup tie. In the 33rd minute with the score at 0–0, Mansfield were awarded a penalty. Nobody on the visiting side wanted to take the kick so captain Staniforth took the responsibility and had his shot saved by Dan Lewis. Arsenal won 2–0. Staniforth stayed until the club entered the League in 1931, but left for Sutton Town in 1932, then had spells at Worksop Town and finally back where he began at Creswell Colliery as player-manager.

A LENGTHY TIE

During 1971–72, a tie in the second round of the Fife and Lothians Cup lasted 126 days. It began on 11 December 1971 when Bonnybridge and Newburgh drew 2–2. The replay was postponed three times because of ground conditions. Eventually Bonnybridge won 2– 0 after extra time. But Newburgh protested that their opponents had fielded an ineligible player. This appeal was upheld, but when the replay was arranged the Bonnybridge pitch was unplayable. Finally it was replayed and Newburgh won. 2–1 after extra time.

ALFRETON FRIGHT

While still members of Division Three in 1969–70, Barrow found themselves drawn away against Alfreton in the first round of the FA Cup. They managed to beat them 2–0 but only at the fourth attempt after 1–1, 0–0 and 2–2 draws.

FLOODLIGHT FAILURE

On 28 November 1955, Carlisle United staged the first FA Cup replay under floodlights between League clubs when they met Darlington. But having drawn 0–0 away in their first round tie, they were beaten 3–1.

GENTLEMEN V PLAYERS?

In the 1903–04 FA Cup, Norwich City beat Lowestoft Town (h) 4–1, Yarmouth Town (a) 2–1, Harwich & Parkeston (a) 4–2 and then drew 1–1 with West Norwood (h) in the third qualifying round. Norwich then scratched to enter the FA Amateur Cup.

MIND OVER MATTER

On 6 January 1934, Halifax Town might have their minds on other things, notably an FA Cup tie at Bolton Wanderers. Playing against Stockport County in the League, they were soon three goals down and appeared to lose interest from that moment. After they had let in ten, Danny Ferguson turned to Hugh Flack and asked, 'How many is that?' Came the reply, 'I don't know, but I think we're losing.' Halifax eventually lost 13–0.

It was a different story at Bolton where they led and were unfortunate not to go two up after hitting a post, when the referee inadvertently got in the way of a Halifax forward who was about to score from the rebound. It proved the turning point and Bolton won 3–1, after Flack had gifted them the equaliser.

SIX-HUNT GUNNERS

Arsenal's heaviest FA Cup defeat is 6–0, a score first inflicted upon them by Sunderland. It happened in 1892–93, the season before they entered the League. Having turned professional in 1891, Arsenal were expelled by the London FA and boycotted by most of the amateur clubs in the south. They had to rely on friendlies. In contrast, Sunderland were League champions, heading for their second title and their Scottish centre-forward Jimmy Millar scored a hat-trick. The next time the sides met in the competition was 80 years later in the semi-final at Hillsborough, Sunderland winning 2–1 and going on to win the cup.

LUCK OF THE IRISH

Bolton Wanderers have never lost to a non-league team in the FA Cup since 1888–89, the inaugural season of the Football League, but they were beaten by an Irish side. Unfortunately, not being one of the 18 teams exempted from the qualifying rounds, and because of the clash with League fixtures, Bolton were forced to field their reserves in the Cup. Their first game was against Hurst and it was drawn 0–0, their opponents scratching before the replay. In the next round Bolton beat West Manchester 9–0 before losing 4–0 away to Linfield Athletic.

NEWCASTLE'S HIC (CUP)

Newcastle United took 420 minutes to dispose of Derby County in the fourth round of the FA Cup on the way to winning the 1924 trophy. They had three 2–2 draws, surviving only with a last minute goal from Stan Seymour in the third of these. Both clubs complained about the referee and he was changed for the fourth meeting which resulted in Newcastle winning the toss for choice of ground and the game 5–3.

ALBION AVERSION

West Bromwich Albion had not lost to a non-league club since before the First World War, prior to losing 4–2 to Woking on 5 January 1991 in the third round at The Hawthorns. Twice previously they had been beaten by both Southampton and Tottenham Hotspur, once by West Ham United when their opponents were in the Southern League. Woking had never beaten a League club or reached the fourth round before.

THE NAVY LARK

A second round FA Amateur Cup tie in 1935 involving HMS Victory and Leytonstone took nine and a half hours to be decided. On Saturday 2 February at Leytonstone the teams drew 0–0 after extra time. The following Saturday there was another goalless draw at Portsmouth. On Wednesday 13 February at Kingstonian's ground, there was a 3–3 draw again after extra time and on Monday 18 February HMS Victory won 5–3 after extra time at the same venue. The score after 90 minutes had been 3–3. But Leytonstone lodged an appeal with the FA, protesting against the result on the grounds that Ordinary Seaman McGinty had been ineligible to play on 18 February. According to Amateur Cup rules governing the qualification of service players, only those who were eligible on dates decided for the playing of the round should be allowed to play in postponed, drawn or replayed matches. McGinty had taken the place of Able Seaman Towle, who had played in the three earlier games. The FA ordered the game to be replayed at Wimbledon on 23 February. HMS Victory won 2–1.

WASHING DAY
A heavy, muddy ground in a Boundary Park FA Cup replay with Crewe Alexandra in December 1949 meant that Oldham Athletic players went through 24 pairs of shorts and 26 jerseys during the game.

Boundary Park, 1949: 'One day we might get a plastic pitch'

FOOTBALLING CRICKETERS

HIGHBURY FLANNELS
A number of Arsenal players have appeared in first-class cricket through the years: Denis Compton, Leslie Compton, George Cox, Ted Drake, Andy Ducat, Joe Hulme, Arthur Milton, Don Roper, Jim Standen, Harry Storer, Ray Swallow. Denis Compton, Ducat and Milton played for England at cricket. In addition Brian Close was on Arsenal's books for a short time. Arsenal chairmen Samuel Hill-Wood and Denis Hill-Wood both played for Derbyshire, Peter Hill-Wood turned out for the Free Foresters.

WILLOW MEN
Ray Swallow, Ian Hall and Ian Buxton played for Derby County and Derbyshire in 1959–60, while three seasons earlier Stuart Leary, Sid O'Linn and Derek Ufton of Charlton Athletic played for Kent and Micky Stewart for Surrey.

DUCKS AND BREAKS
Derby County and England centre-forward Jack Lee took a wicket with the first ball he delivered for Leicestershire in 1947. Plymouth Argyle inside-forward George Dews was out for a duck in all of his first three innings with Worcestershire in 1946.

LOOSE CONNECTION
Brian Close, the Yorkshire and England cricketer, turned professional with Leeds United in February 1949 at 18 and had won England youth international honours. In August 1950 he was transferred to Arsenal but it was not until his move back to Yorkshire with Bradford City in October 1952 that he made his Football League debut.

TIM IN 3-D
Tim Buzaglo, who made the headlines by scoring a hat-trick for Woking in their FA Cup third round tie at West Bromwich Albion on 5 January 1991, had already established himself as an international class cricketer for Gibraltar. Before the 1967 FA Cup Final he had said that he would support the losing team and thus became a Chelsea fan.

BATTING RECORD
Gary Lineker has played for Leicestershire CCC Second XI and is a member of the MCC. He has scored a century for them.

NINETY-MINUTE ALL-ROUNDER
Ten-goal Joe Payne, who set up a Football League record on 13 April 1936 by scoring ten goals as Luton Town beat Bristol Rovers 12–0 in a Division Three (South) match, was also an accomplished cricketer. He played for Bedfordshire from 1937 and in June 1952 he scored 110 in 90 minutes despite having not played for a year.

ALL IN THREES

THE SAINT AND EASY
Ian St John scored a second-half hat-trick in two and a half minutes for Motherwell against Hibernian in an away Scottish League Cup tie on 15 August 1959. Motherwell won 3–1.

THREE FOR BERND
West German international midfield Bernd Schuster was the first player to appear for Spain's three leading clubs: Barcelona, Real Madrid and Atletico Madrid. He spent eight years with Barcelona, two with Real and joined Atletico in 1990.

LEFT-WING BIAS
The first three South Africans to play in post-war FA Cup Finals were Bill Perry (Blackpool 1951, 1953), Des Horne (Wolverhampton Wanderers 1960) and Albert Johanneson (Leeds United 1965). All three were outside-lefts.

JACK THE COUNTY LAD
Jack Lambert, who made his name as a goalscoring centre-forward with Arsenal, actually made his first three appearances for different clubs in his native Yorkshire: Rotherham United 1922– 23, Leeds United 1923–24 and Doncaster Rovers 1924–25.

WELSH WIZARD
Manager Billy McCandless steered three Welsh clubs to promotion from Division Three (South): Newport County in 1939, Cardiff City in 1947 and Swansea Town in 1949.

UNIQUE HAT-TRICKS
George Yardley scored numerous hat-tricks during his career, in Scotland with East Fife and then with Tranmere Rovers. But in December 1970 he emigrated to Australia for the third time.

Edinburgh born forward Tommy Anderson joined Watford from Queen of the South in December 1956 and then played for Bournemouth, Queen's Park Rangers, Torquay United, Stockport County, Doncaster Rovers and Wrexham before going to Australia. He returned to play for Barrow, went back, before a further trip to this country with Watford and then moved to Australia for a third time prior to coming back with Orient.

ORIENTAL RON
In 1963–64 Ron Saunders scored two hat-tricks for Portsmouth against Leyton Orient in separate games. The first was achieved after Portsmouth were three goals down, the second after they had been two behind. The first match was won 6–3, the second 4–3.

ELLAND ROAD TREBLE SHOOTERS
Percy Whipp scored a hat-trick on his debut for Leeds United on 4 November 1922 in a 3–1 win over West Ham United at Elland Road, one of his goals coming from a penalty. On 20 February 1922 Billy Poyntz was married in the morning and scored a hat-trick for Leeds in the afternoon in a 3–0 win over Leicester City. Leeds' Tom Jennings scored three successive hat-tricks in

1926. He had a 3 and two 4's, scoring 11 of the 12 goals Leeds scored. Poyntz had been ordered off the field against Bury on 11 February.

THE NEWRY THREE
In the same week that Newry born Tottenham Hotspur goalkeeper Pat Jennings scored a goal against Manchester United in the 1967 Charity Shield game, two other goalkeepers from Newry also found the net. In the Newry Summer League, Brendan Loughran scored from a penalty for Taylors FC against Hall Rovers and Bobby Woods achieved a similar feat for Drumcashlone against Park View.

CARLISLE REVISITED
Alan Ashman was the first player to score a hat-trick on his League debut for Carlisle United, a feat he performed in a 4–0 win at Rochdale on 18 August 1951. He later became United's manager.

ONE IN THREE
Frank Dudley scored his first three goals of the 1953–54 season for three different clubs in three different divisions. His first was for Southampton against Watford in Division Three (South) on 19 August, the second on 31 October for Cardiff City against Charlton Athletic in Division One, and the third for Brentford against Oldham Athletic in Division Two on Christmas Day.

REVENGE IS THE SPUR
Mike Flanagan had been rejected by Tottenham Hotspur as an amateur player on their books,

and later signed for Charlton Athletic. The first game he played against Spurs was on 15 October 1977 and he scored a hat-trick in a 4–1 win.

BAILLIE BRIDGES
Right-back Joe Baillie made three consecutive appearances for three different clubs. Transferred from Celtic to Wolverhampton Wanderers he made one appearance in two seasons at Molineux before being transferred to Bristol City in June 1956. Later he was with Leicester City and Bradford Park Avenue and completed more than 100 League appearances.

WELSH TOURIST
William Matthews was a centre-half who played three times for Wales, each time with different clubs in different divisions: in April 1921 v Ireland with Liverpool (Division One); in March 1923 v England with Bristol City (Division Three South) and in February 1926 v England with Bradford Park Avenue (Division Three North).

(W) RIGHT TRAINING
Colchester United had three unrelated goalkeepers named Wright in the years immediately after the Second World War: Harry, George and John, who followed each other in the team.

FRANK – IN EARNEST
Tottenham Hotspur centre-forward Frank Osborne scored three consecutive hat-tricks in 1925–26: v Liverpool 24 October (h) won 3–1; v Leicester City 31 October (a) lost 3–5 and v West Ham United 7 November (h) won 4–2.

BOB'S FULL HOUSE

Nottingham Forest lasted longer than any other Football League club in not having a player sent off in the competition during the post-war period. But at the same time they had had other players dismissed in other competitions. Moreover half-back Bob Chapman had been dismissed playing for Forest's 'A' team, the reserves and the first team in a cup-tie.

THREE'S IN EVIDENCE

West Ham United scored three goals in each round of the FA Cup in 1963–64, including the Final. They were also involved in one replay after a 1–1 draw.

REGULAR PARINGS

Southampton and Liverpool met in three consecutive seasons of the FA Cup in the 1920s. In 1923–24 Liverpool won a third round replay 2–0 after a 0–0 draw, in 1924–25 Southampton beat them 1–0 in the fourth round and in 1925–26 Liverpool again won a third round replay following a goalless draw.

THREE IN CHARGE

In 1947–48 Dally Duncan was Luton Town's player-manager, Frank Soo its player-coach, but on the field, centre-half Horace Gager was boss as the team captain.

WOOL CITY GATHERINGS

Jack Padgett's Football League career was restricted to just three games, yet he appeared and scored for both Bradford clubs. He made two appearances for City in 1937–38 and one for Park Avenue in 1938–39.

SOUTHAMPTON REVISITED X 3

Southampton born Tom Parker signed for his local club in 1918, left in 1926 to join Arsenal, was made captain in 1928 and appointed Norwich City manager in 1933. He became Southampton's manager in 1937, only to return to Norwich in 1955. He was appointed Southampton chief scout in 1963.

HIGH MANNING LEVELS

On 13 February 1976 John Manning, the 34-year-old Crewe trainer-coach who had not played a League game for 18 months, was brought back at centre-forward to score a hat-trick in a 4–0 win over Southport.

MR ROCHDALE'S DIARY

Wally Jones represented Rochdale at football, rugby league and cricket. A centre-forward, he played two League games in 1946–47 and scored two goals in one of them, at Stockport County.

THREE DEGREES

Charlie Wilson, a centre-forward, won championship medals in three divisions of the Football League. In 1920 he did so with Tottenham Hotspur in Division Two, in 1924 and again in 1925 with Huddersfield Town in Division One as well as for Stoke City in Division Three (North) in 1927.

IRISH VERSION CORRECT

During a Texaco Cup match in the 1970s, Ballymena full-back Tom Gowdy was cautioned by

Edinburgh referee Eddie Pringle. Three times the official asked the player his name and each time got it wrong. Eventually Gowdy asked the referee to hand over his book and wrote it in himself.

'I give up. You *write it down!'*

A SWITCH IN TIME

DAN, DAN THE VERSATILE MAN
Before Danny Clapton turned professional for Arsenal in 1953 he had been variously a meat porter in Smithfield market, an upholsterer, a fish porter in Billingsgate and a tailor's presser.

DABBLING BROOKS
On 28 September 1938, four days after suffering Bournemouth's then heaviest home defeat 4–0, their goalkeeper Len Brooks disappeared after morning training. He subsequently wrote to the club informing them that

Highbury? This must be the plaice . . .

he was worried over his health, was working in Bristol and had decided to retire from the game. But the following year he signed for Colchester United, then of the Southern League. Bournemouth reported the matter to the FA who suspended him for 28 days and ordered him to repay £48 in wages received from Bournemouth. Brook remained on Bournemouth's open-to-transfer list until 1946.

PARTY GAMES
Annoyed that Greenwich Council had turned down their plans for return to The Valley, Charlton Athletic supporters fought each ward in the local council's elections in 1990 and as The Valley Party achieved a total of 15000 votes. In 1991 they were given permission to return to their old ground.

CHANGE OF EMPHASIS
In June 1931 Mansfield Town secured a place in the Football League at the seventh attempt. They were elected to Division Three (South) with 25 votes, six more than Newport County. In Mansfield's six previous applications they had applied to Division Three (North).

WHITER THAN WHITE
When Don Revie became manager of Leeds United in 1962 he wanted the club to become as outstanding as Real Madrid. He changed the strip to all white.

QUICK MOVER
In December 1957, winger Tony McNamara was transferred from Everton (Division One) to Liverpool (Division Two). In July 1958 he moved to Crewe

Alexandra (Division Four) and in September to Bury (Division Three). In 1959 he found himself out of the League with Runcorn.

PAST CHRISTMAS PRESENT
Middlesbrough were not drawn at home in Football League games on Christmas Day from 1928, when they met Port Vale, until a wartime regional match with Bradford City in 1941.

MOBILE MACAULAY
The shortest time in which a manager ever led clubs in all four divisions was achieved by Archie Macaulay in the 1960s. He was manager of Norwich City from 1957, leaving them when they were in Division Two for West Bromwich Albion of Division One in 1961. In 1963 he switched to Brighton & Hove Albion who quickly slipped from Division Three to Four. As a player he was the first to appear for a relegated Division One team one season and the League championship winners the next: in 1946–47 he went down with Brentford only to win a medal with Arsenal in 1947–48. Not surprisingly the Macaulays, Archie and wife Nessie, moved house 13 times in 21 years.

SINKING FEELING
Scottish centre-forward George Whitelaw changed clubs in four divisions in as many seasons and each time moved down. In 1957–58 he was with Sunderland in Division One and played for them in Division Two the following season. In 1959–60 he played for Queen's Park Rangers and Halifax Town in Division Three and in 1960–61 was with Carlisle United in Division Four.

ON THE SPOT

TREBLE TROUBLES

In a Division Two match on 7 January 1947 at Saltergate, Chesterfield beat Sheffield Wednesday 4–2. Wednesday conceded three penalties in the 56th, 64th and 77th minutes. George Milburn converted all three against Roy Smith as Chesterfield moved from being 2–1 down to winning 4–2. Milburn's first kick was high to the right of Smith, the second on the ground to the right and the third to the left. After the game he told Smith: 'Well, kid, I guess you know now that lightning never strikes in the same place.'

Wednesday also conceded three penalties in another Division Two game at Grimsby Town on 8 October 1949. Stan Lloyd, Grimsby's right-winger scored from the first and third kicks, but Dave McIntosh saved the second by pushing the ball against a post. Grimsby won 4–1.

WHIRLING DERVISH

Swindon Town goalkeeper Sam Burton had something of a reputation as an unconventional penalty stopper in the mid-1950s. During 1953–54 in a Division Three match on 30 January against Southend United, he developed a style of arm-waving antics while Frank Burns prepared to take the kick. The referee was nonplussed and ordered the kick to be retaken. Burns scored and Southend won 3–1. On 4 September 1954 Swindon met Southend again. Burton had already confused Ian Jamieson (Coventry City) and Martin Reagan (Norwich City) into missing penalties. He conceded one against Southend by colliding with Kevin Baron and was still feeling groggy

when Burns rattled in the spot kick in a 4–1 win, Burton having not been in condition to repeat his brand of gamesmanship.

THE TROUBLE WITH HARRY

Brighton & Hove Albion went to Swansea Town for the last match of 1947–48 needing a win to avoid applying for re-election to the Third Division (South). Swansea were awarded a penalty and Dai James, who had never missed from the spot, came up to take it. Harry Baldwin, the Brighton goalkeeper, had saved the last four penalties against him and he made it five with a full length dive in which he caught the ball with both hands. He succeeded in keeping a clean sheet that day, but Brighton could only draw 0–0 and had to go cap in hand to the League. Ironically Albion's top scorer was Tony James with 12 goals.

FILLOL EQUALS EL LOCO

Ubaldo Fillol, the Argentine international goalkeeper, retired at 40 in 1991. In his last match for Velez Sarsfield he saved a penalty in a 2–1 win over River Plate. It was his 26th penalty save and equalled the record of Hugo 'El Loco' Gatti.

VIRTUE ITS OWN. . .

On 8 March 1952 Brighton & Hove Albion beat Walsall 5–1 in a Division Three (South) game. Three minutes from time Jackie Mansell, who had scored from a penalty in the first half, waived his second penalty to allow Brighton inside-left Ken Bennett to complete his hat-trick. But

'Ten to one he puts it high to my left . . .'

Bennett's shot was parried by Walsall goalkeeper Jack Lewis, only for Mansell to follow up and score.

ODDS ON
Oldham Athletic were playing Kidderminster Harriers in an FA Cup tie in 1907 when the referee awarded a penalty against them. He placed the ball on the spot and then discovered there was no goalkeeper. Oldham's custodian Hewitson was behind the goal among the fans, laying odds that they would not score – and they didn't.

AUSTIN FAULTY
In the last game of the 1925–26 season, Manchester City were away to Newcastle United and hoping to register their fifth consecutive win. They needed one point to avoid relegation but Billy Austin missed a penalty, City lost 3–2 and went down.

NOBLE CAUSE
Norman Noble missed a penalty in the last game of the 1958–59 season for Rotherham United and the club missed the Division Four championship and promotion.

TREBLE FAILURE

On 22 September 1973 Notts County missed three attempts at a penalty kick in a Division Two game against Portsmouth at Fratton Park. Kevin Randall's shot was ordered to be retaken because the goalkeeper moved. Don Masson's effort was ruled out because the referee did not signal him to take the kick, then Brian Stubbs failed with the third.

THE FAMOUS FIVE

Five penalty kicks were awarded in the replayed FA Cup tie between Iswich Town and Lowestoft Town on 21 October 1936. Ipswich scored all theirs, Lowestoft scored one and missed another of their penalties. Ipswich won 7–1 after a 1–1 draw in the second qualifying round.

FORD PERFECT

On 1 September 1973, Don Ford of Hearts scored a hat-trick of penalties in a 3–2 win away to Morton.

PENALTY CAUSE

In 1982–83 Portsmouth missed nine penalty kicks. Six different players were involved before Kevin Dillon broke the jinx by scoring twice from the spot in a 2–2 draw with Reading on the Saturday following Good Friday.

SUPPORT YOUR LOCAL TEAM

During the 1953–54 season the Aldershot programme attempted to explain the club's poor attendances:

'Population of Aldershot and District 50000

Less people over 65 not interested in football, have rheumatics or other old age complaints 15000.

Less babes in arms and other toddlers 10000

Less people in hospital, lunatic asylums, public houses, services or otherwise indisposed 8000.

Less husbands on allotments or at home doing housework and wives out shopping 12000.

People in jail 250.

Less shop assistants and others working during football hours 3904.

Less gatemen, officials, police and others who do not pay for admission 150.

Less people who have acquired complimentary tickets 200.

Less people who climbed over railings 482.

Leaving 14: manager, trainer, secretary, 11 players.

Just as well that the visitors bring spectators with them!'

FIRST THINGS FIRST

TRUST MERSEYSIDE
The idea of teams entering the field in pairs was first introduced in derby matches on Merseyside between Liverpool and Everton.

MINI-SOCCER BLOW
The table soccer game Subbuteo attempted to become an Olympic sport in 1992 but was turned down.

VAGUE ORIGINS
There are no records of games played by Bolton Wanderers prior to 1879 due to reports of Association Football not being carried in newspapers. The club played against rugby clubs in their early days, one half under the handling code, the other under soccer rules. But even in 1894 the *Football Field*, a Bolton Saturday evening sports paper, claimed that Christ Church – the club's previous name – followed the rugby code for two years from the club's inception, whereas other reports suggest that they played half and half as mentioned.

BANDED ABOUT
The first Queen's Park team wore armbands as their only distinguishing piece of uniform.

DESIGNER DEBUT
Everton were the first club in Great Britain to introduce a stripe down the seams of their shorts.

BIASED REPORTING
The first radio football commentary was undertaken by George Allison on 23 April 1927. He was an Arsenal director at the time, but still covered the Arsenal v Cardiff City FA Cup Final. His assistant was Derek McCulloch, later to become famous as 'Uncle Mac' on *Children's Hour*

WOOL CITY FIRST
In 1963–64 the long-since defunct Bradford Park Avenue and Bradford City became the first two teams from one City to have met each other in four divisions of the Football League.

ANIMAL MAGIC
Wolverhampton Wanderers were the first former members of Division Three (North) to win the Football League championship. Relegated to the former in 1923, Wolves won the Division One title in 1953–54.

MODEST START
Pat Bonner, Celtic's Republic of Ireland international goalkeeper in the 1990 World Cup, played for Leicester City in the 1975–76 FA Youth Cup.

BLUE MOVER
The first University Blue to turn professional was Oxford's centre-forward George Ansell, who joined Brighton & Hove Albion in August 1932. He later

played for Norwich City and Southampton.

BEGINNERS LUCK
Three times when Manchester City won the FA Cup they included a player who had made his Football League debut that season: Frank Swift in 1934, Jack Dyson in 1956 and Tommy Booth in 1969. City had scored 31 goals on the way to Wembley in 1926 but lost 1–0 to Bolton Wanderers in the final and were relegated to Division Two the same season.

WHISTLER MOTHER
On 5 September 1976, Mrs Pat Dunne became the first woman to referee an official game between male teams. It was in the Dorset County Sunday League.

ORIGINAL MARINERS
Grimsby Town were one of the original 12 members of Division Two in 1892, one of 22 in Division Three (South) in 1920 and one of 20 in Division Three (North) the following season.

'I bet she uses Charmony hair spray'

FAMILIAR FOES

The first two clubs to meet each other in Divisions One, Two, Three and Four were Bradford Park Avenue and Oldham Athletic. They completed the series in 1958–59.

ANCIENT AND MODERN

Long-term contracts are nothing new in the game. In the early 1890s Fred Spiksley signed a three-year contract with Sheffield Wednesday.

CUTTING EDGE

On 5 April 1986 Jimmy Glass, 16, scored on his debut for Arbroath against Albion Rovers and helped his team to win 2–0.

FAMOUS FIRST

Notts County were the first team to score a goal against Queen's Park, on 8 March 1875.

NUMBER ONE

Airdrie claim to have been the first Scottish club to number their players.

NEEDY START

The Celtic club was formed in November 1887, its main object being to raise funds for meals for the needy children of the East End of Glasgow. Their first game was a friendly against Rangers in May 1888 which they won 5–2 at the first Celtic Park ground.

A BLOOMING SWEDE

In 1991 two Bolivians David Saracho (Blooming) and Joaquin Vargas (Florida) became the first South Americans to join a Swedish club when they signed for Division Two team Hacken.

RAY CHARLES ON SONG

In 1984–85 Montrose achieved their first major trophy in 106 years by winning the Division Two championship. Goalkeeper Ray Charles was unbeaten in 18 of the matches played.

TRIAL BY JURY

In 1952 Arthur Jefferson, the Aldershot full-back, brought a trialist to the club. In a practice game the 21-year-old was put at left-back and manager Gordon Clark decided to play at outside-right to oppose him. Four times in the opening minutes the beefy young man floored Clark. He turned out to be Arthur's younger brother Stan. He was signed.

ROWE IN-AHEAD

Arthur Rowe, in his first two seasons as Tottenham Hotspur manager, took the club to the Division Two championship in 1949–50 and the Division One title in 1950–51.

ONE TOUCH

Peter McParland (Aston Villa) scored with his first kick 40 seconds after the start of his international debut for Ireland, versus Wales on 31 March 1954, against Jack Kelsey, the Welsh goalkeeper making his first appearance.

NO PIGEON TOES

Jackie Robinson made his league debut for Sheffield Wednesday on 22 April 1935 against West Bromwich Albion at inside-left

in place of Ronnie Starling, whose boots he borrowed for the occasion. When Starling was transferred, Robinson took his place permanently – with his own footwear.

RAISBECK'S SPECS
Liverpool's Alex Raisbeck was believed to be the first player to appear regularly in first-class football wearing spectacles. He made more than 340 League and Cup appearances for the club between 1898 and 1909.

HEAD HUNTERS
Eyemouth made history by beating Cowdenbeath 3–0 in the Scottish Cup third round on 27 February 1960 to become the first non-league club to reach the last eight. In the fourth round they were narrowly beaten 2–1 by Division One Kilmarnock.

BACK TO THE FUTURE
On 6 February 1960 when West Ham United beat Chelsea 4–2 in a Division One game, John Lyall, 19, was making his debut as left-

back for the Hammers, while Terry Venables, 17, was introduced for the first time by the visitors.

BEGINNER'S LUCK
On 31 March 1973, Crystal Palace beat Chelsea 2–0. It was the first time in 32 attempts that they had defeated a London club in a League game. It was also Malcolm Allison's first game as manager.

YOUR NUMBER'S UP
Numbered placards for substitutes were first used in Football League games in 1975.

FIRST ON THE ISLAND
On 17 May 1948, Sheffield United played Sheffield Wednesday in Douglas, Isle of Man, in a friendly. It was the first game between professionals ever staged on the island. The result was a 2–2 draw, in front of 8000 spectators.

RESTRICTED OUTPUT

France might well have won the 1958 World Cup had it not been for injury to Thadee Cisowski. Born in Laski, Poland, in 1927, he later became a naturalised Frenchman. He was also one of the most injury-prone players of all time, Cisowski was out injured 37 times, and had seven operations, two of them on his knees. Even at the age of 17 working in the coal mines, he broke his leg in an accident.

He joined Metz in the late 1940s and gradually made a name for himself as a goalscorer. In 1949–50 he scored 17 League goals and the following season was top scorer in Division Two with 23 goals. He moved on to Racing Club de Paris and injuries apart, his next most successful season was 1953–54 when he scored 34. In 1955–56 he was top in Division One with 31 and again in 1956–57 with 33. In 1958–59 he led again with 30 and in 1959–60 was second highest marksman on 27. Later he played for Nantes and Valenciennes. To judge the influence his absences had on his goalscoring, from 1947–48 to 1960–61 his seasonal totals were: 3, 15, 17, 23, 10, 13, 34, 9, 31, 33, 9, 30, 27, 9.

During this period he did manage to make 13 appearances for France, spread over a period of seven years from 1951 to 1958. Among the 11 goals he scored were five in a 6–3 win over Belgium in a World Cup qualifying match on 11 November 1956, which established a French record. His goals came in the 13th, 15th, 44th, 72nd and 88th minutes. Two days afer his five-goal effort he scored two against Honved then a hat-trick versus Sochaux in the league. But he was always injured when it came to playing in the World Cup final tournaments of 1954 and 1958.

UNIQUE
SITUATIONS

GUNNERS ALL-ROUND
In 1951 Arsenal furnished both centre-halves to an England (Leslie Compton) v Wales (Ray Daniel) international. In 1963–64 they completed the quartet by supplying Scotland (Ian Ure) v Northern Ireland (Terry Neill).

COUNTRY BEFORE CLUB
When Hibernian centre-half Johnny Paterson was serving in the Black Watch during the Second World War, his photograph appeared on recruiting posters.

FLY BOY
Tony Pawson, writer, author, Kent County Cricketer and an Oxford Blue at soccer and cricket, played for Pegasus, Charlton Athletic and England Amateurs. In 1984 he became world fly-fishing champion.

JUST ONE OUTING
The circumstances of New Brighton manager Neil McBain being forced to play himself in goal against Hartlepools United in an emergency at the age of 51 years 4 months on 15 March 1947 are well documented. But the other player to be commandeered that day was Nicholas Evans. A 21-year-old who played for Heselden at inside-left in the Hartlepool and District League, he was the son of Nicol Evans, a Hartlepools official. He played creditably at outside-right in his only Football League appearance.

FLAG WAVER
Steve Bloomer of Derby County acted as a linesman at Elland Road during a friendly between Leeds City and Derby on 25 March 1905, the season before City were elected to the Football League.

YOUNGEST TO SIGN
When Ray Lambert signed amateur forms for Liverpool on 23 January 1936 he was only 13 years 188 days old. Although he turned professional in July 1939 he had to wait until after the Second World War for his Football League debut, though he had played in wartime Regional League football for the club.

FEMALE HISTORY
Kim George, a 28-year-old maths teacher from Bognor, became the first woman to officiate in the 116-year history of the FA Cup when she refereed the Shoreham v Eastbourne preliminary round tie on 3 September 1988.

RED CARD
On 27 October 1990, Ben Rowe of Exeter City was sent off against Fulham in a Division Three game for dissent while acting as substitute and still sitting in the dugout.

ANOTHER FINE MESS . . .
At the time of their withdrawal from the Football League in

March 1962, Accrington Stanley had played 33 matches in Division Four. Of these they had won just 5, drawn 8 and lost 20. They had scored 19 goals and conceded 60. Their final match was on Friday 2 March and they were beaten 4–0 at Crewe Alexandra. The team was: A Smith; Forrester, Gregory, Pickup, Wilson, Hamilton, Devine, Bennett, W Smith, Ferguson and Mulvey. Their record was expunged from the table.

OUT OF CONTEXT
Southend United's 1955 summer tour of Malta produced a newspaper poster there which read: *SOUTHEND UNITED'S ARRIVAL* and in smaller letters underneath *SCOTLAND YARD RE-SHUFFLE*.

AA HOME START
Archie Aikman, a Scottish born centre-forward, had a number of clubs during his career including Manchester City and Rangers, although he did not manage to play competitively for either of them. After spells with Hearts and St Mirren he moved to Falkirk, who transferred him to Manchester City. But he was badly hurt in a car crash and his career seemed to have ended. He returned home and played a few games for Stenhousemuir. Rangers signed him in 1952 but he spent three months without getting a game and went back to Stenhousemuir.

MIDGET MARVELS
Preston North End's five-man forward line in the 1938 FA Cup Final had an aggregate height of only 27ft 8in. Preston beat Huddersfield Town 1–0 after extra time.

TAYLOR'S MADE
In 1952 Aldershot signed right-winger George Taylor from Hamilton Academical. He had been born in Edinburgh and developed with Bonnyrigg Rose. The following year the club secured a goalkeeper called George Taylor from Hamilton Academical, who had been born in Edinburgh and played for Bonnyrigg Rose. Winger Taylor moved to Guildford City early in 1953–54 and goalkeeper Taylor was transferred to Hartlepool United in January 1954. In October 1953 Aldershot had transferred goalkeeper Joe Houston to Hamilton.

CHASE FOR BATES
Ken Bates, the Chelsea chairman, played for Chase of Chertsey as a defender when that club was Arsenal's nursery in the late 1940s.

A KNIGHT HODDER
In 1961 the Stockport County centre-half Ken Hodder was made a Knight of the Road in recognition of his considerate driving.

TEENAGE IRRITANT HERO HURDLE
Jimmy Moncrief, who played as a teenage amateur centre-forward with Halifax Town in the years immediately after the Second World War, was an outstanding youngster. At the tender age of 13 he was something of a legend but also an obstacle to opponents as outside-right for Heptonstall in the Halifax and District League. Several teams complained that he was too young to be playing against them. He later won his Blue at Oxford University and also appeared at wing-half.

FOREST ATTRACTION
In November 1931, Bill Anderson went to Nottingham Forest on two months' trial from County Durham. Later, while playing for Barnsley, he suffered a double leg-fracture playing against Forest and in November 1966 left Lincoln City to become assistant manager at the City ground.

QPR UK OK?
Queen's Park Rangers' four immediate pre-war managers were: Archie Mitchell (English), Mick O'Brien (Irish), Billy Birrell (Scottish) and Ted Vizard (Welsh).

FORM OF EVIDENCE
Trevor Ford had a career as a goalscoring centre-forward which lasted 18 years and began during the Second World War. Throughout his varied service he kept unsigned the registration form that Arsenal sent him, to scotch rumours that the Highbury club had lost interest after giving him a trial. But they just wanted him to sign amateur forms.

LOW EBB
Southend United were the last club to lose continuous membership of Division Three since its formation in 1920, when relegated in May 1966.

HAROLD'S MOVES
Harold Wightman had a busy time in the mid-1930s. He was manager of Luton Town from 1931 to October 1935 when he resigned and became a scout for Derby County in November. In January 1936 he took over as manager of Mansfield Town for a

brief spell before taking up a similar position with Nottingham Forest from May until 1939.

ONE-ARMED GAMBIT
Thought to be the only player to appear in international football with one arm was Robert Schlienz. He was a right-half or centre-half and captained Stuttgart in the 1950s. He won three caps for West Germany including one against England on 26 May 1956.

INNOVATION
During a floodlit friendly at Elland Road in 1954 between Leeds United and a team of ex-internationals, the veterans were awarded a penalty. Peter Doherty took the kick but instead of shooting for goal, pushed the ball to his right a few yards for Raich Carter to run in and score, a ruse quite within the rules but rarely attempted. While manager of Doncaster Rovers in the 1950s, Doherty often confused the opposition by giving his forwards different shirt numbers from those usually accepted in those days.

THEIR HEARTS RIGHT THERE
'It's a long way to Tipperary', so ran the First World War song. It was for the Moulson brothers who were born there. Con was a centre-half with Grimsby Town, Bristol City, Lincoln City and Notts County in the 1930s. He won five caps for the Republic of Ireland. Brother George was a goalkeeper who played for Grimsby, Lincoln and Peterborough United. He actually signed for Grimsby in 1936 from the Army. He made his first senior appearance in the 1939 FA Cup semi-final against Wolverhampton Wanderers but

was carried off injured in the early stages. He did manage wartime appearances for the club and as a guest for Lincoln, but had to wait until after the Second World War for two more FA Cup games in 1945–46 and it was not until April 1947 that he made his League debut! He moved to Lincoln, winning a Division Three (North) championship medal in 1948, and the following year joined Peterborough United. But he also made three Republic of Ireland appearances in 1948. Coincidentally, George was born on the day the 1914–18 war broke out.

TEMPORARY ARRANGEMENT?
Portakabin, a local York firm, sponsored the club's newly-formed Under-16 team during the 1990–91 season.

WORTH THE WEIGHT
Jackie Sewell became the first player literally to be worth his weight in gold. On 15 March 1951, 210 minutes before the transfer deadline, he was sold by Notts County to Sheffield Wednesday for £35000. He weighed 12st at the time and gold was £12 8s 0d a troy ounce, 12 troy ounces to the pound.

CALLING BLUEBOTTLE
Comedian Peter Sellers became an honorary vice-President of Wood Green Town in 1959. Chairman Ernie Kingston was a radio ham with a radio-telephone installed in his car. He discovered that Sellers had a similar gadget and contacted him. Sellers agreed to the offer. His call sign was Blue 21, Kingston's was Blue 61.

ACE COLLECTION
Jim Langley, the Leeds United, Brighton & Hove Albion, Fulham and Queen's Park Rangers defender, had a cigarette card collection of more than 20000 and often exhibited them publicly.

NO HOME BANKERS
Arsenal, Notts County, Blackpool and Loughborough Town all share the record of having managed just one home win in a Football League season. Blackpool's one success was 6–0 against Newcastle United on 22 October 1966 in Division One.

HINES 47 VARIETY
Though it has been claimed that Derek Hines made his trial debut for Southend United reserves at the age of only 13, he was actually 14. Born on 8 February 1931, it could not have been in 1944 as Southend did not resume playing until after the war. Later Hines played 299 League games for Leicester City for whom he had signed as an amateur in 1947. He finished his League career with Shrewsbury Town.

MEDICAL GUNNERS
Four professional doctors have played for Arsenal during their history: Leigh Richmond Roose, James Paterson, James Marshall and Kevin O'Flanagan. Two others guested during the last war.

SUPPORTING ACTION
Aldershot-based computer company Datrontech announced a unique sponsorship package in January 1991, advertising on the Aldershot players' jock straps.

TEAM WITH NO NAME

Manchester United's first match following the Munich air disaster was against Sheffield Wednesday on 19 February 1958 in a FA Cup fifth round tie. There were no names printed for United's team on the programme, as its composition was in doubt right up to the kick-off. United won 3–0 before a crowd of 59 848 at Old Trafford.

BOUNCING CZECHS?

At the winter pause half-way through the 1990–91 season, West Bohemian border club Union Cheb led the Division One table in Czechoslovakia, but only 1928 saw their 1–0 home win against Nitra. The last round of eight games produced 15 goals, 30 yellow cards and only 17641 frozen fans.

BOXING CLEVER

Although Dundee United found it impossible to play in the 1940–41 season for one year, one major sporting event was held at Tannadice Park on New Year's Day 1941. Jim Brady of Dundee outpointed Kid Tanner for the Empire bantamweight boxing title.

GAMES OF TWO HALVES

Dave Mycock's benefit game for Halifax Town in 1952 was something different. Halifax played Halifax Rugby League club. In the first half they played soccer, second half rugger. The soccer score was 1–1, the rugger game was 17–17. The Rugby League side were awarded a penalty on the stroke of half-time to equalise and Halifax Town were given a penalty kick in front of the posts to draw level near the end.

NAFF DAF

The lowest attendance recorded at a match involving Football League teams in 1990–91 was on 27 November 1990 when only 409 saw Chester City beat Bury 2–0 in a Leyland Daf preliminary round tie at Macclesfield.

CLASS WITH RESERVATIONS

When Arsenal won the League Championship in 1937–38 they did so with 52 points, only 16 more than the bottom club.

SWINGING SIXTIES

Carlisle United supporters could not have become bored in the 1960s. Between 1962 and 1966 they appeared in five different divisions in successive seasons, moving from Division Four to Three, back to Four, up to Three, and then on to Division Two.

'IRISH' HOME GAME

When Peter Farrell scored for the Republic of Ireland against England at Goodison Park on 21 September 1949, he became the only international to score an away goal on his home ground as an Everton player.

TEN AT PENNYDARREN

In December 1951 the FA Cup winners met the Welsh Cup winners in a friendly at Pennydarren Park, Merthyr. Newcastle United beat Merthyr Tydfil 6–4.

TRAINED

In November 1985 Sir Stanley Matthews unveiled a Pullman coach at Euston named after him.

MORRIS PRANCING
During the 1950s a team in the Kettering Amateur League was called Mrs Morris' Club. The second team was Mrs Morris' Reserves.

HANDY ANDY
In 1967 Notts County appointed Andy Beattie to become the first manager to be in charge of as many as eight different League clubs.

CITY LIGHTS
Brechin is the smallest place in Great Britain with a professional football team. The Angus city has a population of only 7000, qualifying as a city by virtue of its cathedral.

'HOWELLS' OF APPROVAL
It was claimed that 'Rabbi' Howell was the only full-blooded Romany to play soccer for England. Allegedly born in a caravan, Howell signed for Liverpool from Sheffield United and played twice for England, once when a Liverpool player against Scotland in 1899. Some sources have said that Howell was of Jewish descent, which might have been derived from his first name.

UNIQUE HOMING BEES
Since Brentford won all 21 of their home Division Three (South) fixtures in 1929–30, no other club has achieved a similar 100 percent record in any Football League season.

UNITED – YOU FALL
Bristol Rovers can claim to have beaten a First Division Manchester United side in both of the principal cup competitions. They won 4–0 in the FA Cup third round at Eastville on 7 January 1956 and 2–1 in a League Cup third round replay at Old Trafford on 11 October 1972.

EXCITING CLIMAX
On 19 April 1986 Hamilton Academical had won promotion from Division One and Alloa had been relegated, but all other teams in the division were still involved in either promotion or relegation.

HALTING TIME
On 20 January 1990 British Rail opened Ramsline Halt station within a few hundred yards of the Baseball Ground at Derby, for the benefit of visiting supporters. The project cost £320 000 of which BR contributed just £5000.

LIMITED RECALL
During 1989–90 Walsall commemorated the most famous day in the club's history – 14 January 1933 when they beat Arsenal 2–0 in the third round of the FA Cup – by producing a limited edition of 1000 replica copies of that matchday programme. Each was individually numbered and signed personally by Gilbert Alsop, the sole survivor of the game and one of its goalscorers.

BETTER LATE
On 17 February 1973 West Bromwich Albion lost 2–1 at West Ham United to a goal in the 96th minute. Referee Kerkhoff added seven minutes for time-wasting.

STAR SWANS

When Swansea Town beat Lincoln City 3–1 on 16 April 1955, they broke a club record by fielding nine full internationals and two international reserves. Len and Ivor Allchurch, Harry Griffiths, Terry Medwin, Cliff Jones, John and Mel Charles and John King were Welsh caps, Arthur Willis an England international, while Tom Kiley and Dai Thomas had both been Welsh reserves.

TOPSY-TURVEY

On 11 March 1978 referee Alan Turvey sent off two players in the West Ham United v Wolverhampton Wanderers game, having dismissed two others at Queen's Park Rangers on Boxing Day and two more at Fulham a few weeks later.

SWAN UPPING (2)

Terry Medwin, John Charles, Trevor Ford, Ivor Allchurch and Harry Griffiths were all born in Swansea and played for Swansea Town. They comprised the forward line for Wales v Ireland in Belfast on 15 April 1953.

FOREST ROW

On 25 March 1950, Scarborough beat Nottingham Forest reserves 2–0 at the City Ground in a Midland League game. Forest then completed 71 unbeaten home games, winning 62 and drawing 9, scoring 237 goals and conceding 47, before losing 3–2 to York City reserves, the bottom club, three and a half years later.

THE OVAL BALL GAME

One of the first Football League players to claim to have played on the famous Oval enclosure at Sydney, Australia – but not at cricket – was Len Quested. While stationed there during the war he played on the ground as a centre-forward for the Royal Navy in the Sydney Soccer League. Later he served Fulham and Huddersfield Town as a left-half.

CHARITY BEGINS AWAY

In the years immediately after the last war, a referee or linesman in the Football League could charge a meal allowance if his appointment necessitated travel of 80 railway miles. One claimant was informed by the club that his home was 79¾ miles away and refused to pay. On a matter of principle the official approached the railway authorities and found that the distance was 80½. He informed the club, who paid up. He gave the sum to charity.

NEVER ON SUNDAY

On 30 December 1970 Coventry City applied to the Football League for permission to play four experimental League games in March on Sundays. The request was turned down. On 14 June 1971 arrangements were made to stage games on Friday.

SMALL HANDLING CHARGE

When England beat Malta 5–0 at Wembley on 12 May 1971, goalkeeper Gordon Banks only touched the ball four times, all from back passes.

BEARDED WONDER

On 16 September 1972, Jimmy Hill, ex-Coventry City manager and TV commentator and a qualified referee, took over from linesman Dennis Drewitt who tore a leg muscle during the Arsenal v Liverpool Division One game at Highbury.

LIGHTING-UP TIME
In November 1972, linesmen at a Tommy Lawton testimonial changed into luminous tunics as an experiment after complaints by referees that they could not pick out their linesmen in floodlight games.

OFF THEIR TROLLEYS
After extensive wartime damage to Home Park, Plymouth Argyle's ground, two trams were used as miniature stands for directors and officials. Despite later rebuilding in the early 1950s, they were still in use, one as headquarters for the Supporters Club, another as the drying room for the groundstaff.

NO PULLING POWER
In 1928 a competition involving Partick Thistle, Third Lanark, Celtic, Queen's Park, Rangers and Clyde was won by Partick who beat Rangers 2–0 in the final before a crowd of only 5000. The tournament was called the Dental Cup.

Full up on top and inside

LEFT AND (W)RIGHT

Billy Wright never refused to sign autographs. However, it may have been easier for him to do so than others. He was ambidextrous and often signed two books at a time.

ALL FOR ONE, BUT . . .

In 1962–63 eleven different Tottenham Hotspur players were capped but they never appeared together as a Spurs team. Jimmy Greaves, Ron Henry, Maurice Norman and Bobby Smith played for England, Bill Brown, Dave Mackay and John White for Scotland, Mel Hopkins, Cliff Jones and Terry Medwin for Wales and Danny Blanchflower for Northern Ireland.

CHARIOTS OF FIRE

Between the wars, two professional footballers who won the Powderhall Handicap at Edinburgh were Bolton Wanderers left-winger Tom Eatock and Liverpool full-back Jim Harley.

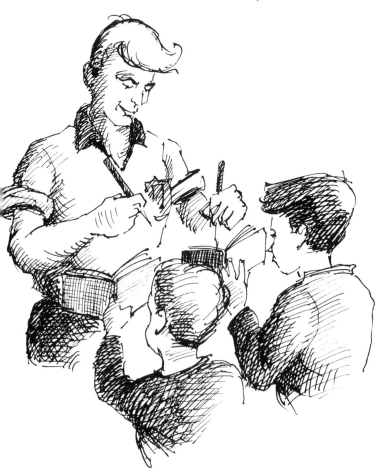

Look, mum – both hands

BARGAIN BUY

In July 1975 Southend United announced that they would print their own club programme at a cost of just 5p to the supporters.

GETTING THE BIRD

In August 1978 Oxford City signed a sponsorship deal with the Post Office giving them the 'Buzby' telephone symbol on their shirts.

PAST DAYS OF POMPEY

Between 1946–47 and 1955–56, Portsmouth and Everton met in 13 Division One matches and Pompey won them all. After losing 1–0 at Goodison Park on 14 September 1946 it was not until 10 November 1956 that Everton managed to avoid defeat in a 2–2 draw on their own ground again.

NOCTURNAL HABITS.

In their early days Everton were known as 'The Moonlight Dribblers'. Their players trained at night, often under the light of the moon.

OF HUMAN BOND-AGE?

In 1959–60 the Showbiz XI included comedian Dave King, singer Des O'Connor on the right-wing and film star Sean Connery at inside-left.

WINSOME SINNERS

Bury wingers Dave Robbie, a Scot, and Englishman Wally Amos appeared together from 1923–24 to 1934–35, but in 1959–60 the Northampton pair Jack English and Tom Fowler had occupied both flanks for 14 successive seasons.

WALLY'S FOLLY

In June 1928, Wally Betteridge was appointed player-coach by Crystal Palace having been signed from Peterborough. He made one first team appearance at right-back on 27 October 1928 at Northampton, where Palace suffered an 8–1 defeat. At the end of the season Palace were pipped for promotion by Charlton Athletic on goal average. Northampton finished third, two points behind Palace as one of four clubs on the same total. In August 1929 Betteridge joined Loughborough.

CUP CURSES

Early in the 1900s, a gypsy woman reading the palm of a Sunderland player said that his club would never win the FA Cup until a Scotswoman sat on the throne. Sunderland finally achieved this success in 1937, by which time the Queen was a Scot.

MEMORIES

There used to be a Bartram Gate at Charlton's The Valley ground and an HC club in the memory of Herbert Chapman. Grimsby had a Bestall Street to honour Jackie Bestall and Walsall's former ground Fellows Park was named after their former chairman Herbert Fellows.

LOCAL HAMMER'S IMPACT

In 1959–60 the only manager among the 92 Football League clubs born in his local area was Ted Fenton of West Ham United.

SOUTH AFRICAN REPRESENTATIVES

On 12 March 1956 an unofficial international was played at Ibrox

Give us a wave before you go

Park between a Scottish XI and South Africa, the opposition being derived from players with English and Scottish League clubs. The Scots won 2–1 before a crowd of 60000.

FLAGGING FORTUNE
On 31 October 1970 a linesman in the Liverpool v Wolverhampton Wanderers match pulled a muscle and was replaced by J Collihole, a Watford referee who was watching his last match before emigrating to Australia.

DUAL ROLES
In 1959–60 Brian Bruce, a 19-year-old left-back, was employed on Liverpool's groundstaff at the same time as he was playing for Southport.

MONEY MATTERS

ADDING MACHINE
On 8 September 1990 Chesterfield unveiled their new electronic turnstile counting system covering 35 turnstiles at a cost of £15000.

PEOPLE'S CHOICE
Alan Mackin, East Stirling's general manager, owns a restaurant and nightclub and drives a Porsche. But he still pays at the turnstiles.

HOLIDAY IN
In 1913 when Arsenal obtained a 21-year lease for £20000 from the Ecclesiastical Commissioners for the Highbury ground, the club agreed not to stage games either on Good Friday or Christmas Day. This restriction was not lifted until 1925 when a further £64000 was paid.

AMATEUR STATUS
On 16 October 1970 Andy McCulloch, a Queen's Park Rangers amateur forward, turned professional. The following day he scored a goal in a 5–2 win over Birmingham City. But he was not paid, because the Football League's stipulation was registration for a minimum of 48 hours.

FLAGGING CASH
When Doncaster Rovers played an away game in Division Two against Bradford City on 14 March 1936, their 12th man was George Flowers, father of Ron Flowers who was later an England international with Wolverhampton Wanderers. A linesman failed to appear and Flowers took over, receiving £1 11s 6d as a fee.

TRAINING GROUND.
The Great Western Railway wanted the Stamford Bridge ground of Chelsea as a marshalling yard in 1905, but the handsome offer was turned down.

WEAK BUT STRONG
Newcastle United won an away Division One game at Bristol City 3–0 on 25 April 1910 and were fined £100 by the Football League for fielding a weak team. They had used their reserves because they were due to play Barnsley in an FA Cup final replay three days later. Newcastle had also been similarly fined in 1906 and were to be in 1924.

MUSTAFA PLAYER
In 1961 a Turkish club in Istanbul were hard up. Their centre-forward Ridvan Sracoglu withdrew his life savings and presented them to the club.

SHORTT CHANGE
On 28 November 1925, Stenhousemuir goalkeeper Joe Shortt was offered £50 to lose the game against bottom of the table Broxburn United. He reported the matter and after Stenhousemuir had won 6–2, a bookmaker was subsequently charged and received a three-month prison sentence.

DIMINISHING RETURNS

In 1960–61 Leeds United signed John McGugan, a centre-half from St Mirren, for £15000. They played him in only one Division Two game then transferred him to Tranmere Rovers for around a third of the fee. Ian McFarlane left Chelsea for Leicester City in 1958 for £9000, played one game then moved to Bath City for nothing.

COSTLY AMATEUR

Before Jimmy Adam turned professional with Luton Town in July 1953 he had already cost Hibernian £25. A Scot from Glasgow he made his Football League debut as a winger for Aldershot in 1950–51. He drifted to Spennymoor from where Luton signed him. But on 14 January 1953, Hugh Shaw the Hibernian manager was severely censured and fined for playing Adam at outside-left while he was still on the books of Berwick Rangers.

CONTENTED WINGER

Northern Ireland international winger Ian Stewart turned down a £100-a-week pay rise with Queen's Park Rangers in 1984 on the grounds that he was living in a boarding house, unmarried and was quite happy with life. He had left school at 16 and at one time was glad of £10-a-week supplementary benefit while out of work.

CONSTRUCTIVE PLAYER

Carlisle United inside-forward Billy Robson, 28, was signed from Workington in November 1959. He was one of three brothers who were partners in a building contract firm and had just signed a contract worth £6 million.

BANGU'S A FORTUNE

In 1984 a 65-year-old mathematics professor left Bangu, a club near Rio in Brazil, £250000 in his will. The reason? He had once fallen in love during Carnival time with a young girl in the little town and having no relatives, decided to remember the local club.

FINE REWARD

On 26 April 1971 Liverpool drew 2–2 away to Manchester City in Division One but were fined a then record £7500 for fielding a weakened team.

COMMON MARKET

In August 1984 the wrangle over Scot Gordon Strachan's transfer to an English club was finally settled after a German team had claimed his signature. Moreover the dispute was resolved in France. He joined Manchester United from Aberdeen in a £500 000 move while Cologne were given £100 000 compensation by the Scottish club following the meeting in Paris.

WINDOW SHOPPER

Because football clubs had subscribed only £60 of the £300 required for a Duncan Edwards church memorial window at St Francis Church at Dudley, Sidney Terry, a Manchester United fan, donated the remainder. He had missed the Munich air disaster because of a cold.

INVESTMENT RETURN?

Roy Pritchard joined Aston Villa from Wolverhampton Wanderers in February 1955 for £6000. He played only three League games before being transferred to Notts County for £2000 in October 1957.

RING OF NO CONFIDENCE
In 1959 in Italy a soccer pool ticket worth the equivalent of £1000 was left by a punter inside a telephone directory for safekeeping. While he was away from his Turin home, the telephone company removed the old directory and replaced it with the new edition. The punter was left to search through 235000 pages in 178499 old telephone directories.

ENTERPRISE ZONE
In 1886 hard-up Blackburn Rovers organised a draw with tickets at 6d (2½p) each. First prize was a newly built cottage on the New Bank Road valued at £140. Other prizes included a piano, watches, a sewing machine and a wringer (hand-powered washing machine).

A NOT (E) ABLE SAVE
Arsenal beat Newcastle United 2–1 at Highbury in a Division Two game on 28 November 1953. In the dying seconds the Arsenal goalkeeper Jack Kelsey

Not another wrong number

made a brilliant one-handed save from Bobby Mitchell. The following day Kelsey received an anonymous £5 note from a spectator for 'the greatest save I have ever seen'.

WISE INVESTMENT?
In August 1982 Aldershot took out insurance *against* gaining promotion.

'PENNY' LANE
Joe 'Charlie' Lane played for Watford and was player-coach to Ferencvaros in Hungary where he scored twice from outside the area in a friendly against Sunderland. They signed him, and in November 1913 he was transferred on to Blackpool for a modest fee. He scored 37 goals for them and in March 1920 Birmingham paid £3600 for his signature. Those days clubs were allowed to pay a percentage of the fee to the player. It was usually 10%, but Lane asked for one-third and was given it. This caused the Football League to change the rule, removing the clause about share of the transfer fee and replacing it with an accrued share of benefit. Lane later played for Millwall and coached Barcelona. At the age of 42 he was still playing for a Watford printing works. At the height of his career it was said he wore outdoor shirts only once before handing them on to other players.

FEAST OF FOOTBALL

These post-war Football League players should be capable of producing some acceptable fare.

GERRY CAKEBREAD	Brentford
MEL SAGE	Gillingham, Derby County
TREVOR PEEL	Bradford PA
GUY BUTTERS	Tottenham Hotspur, Portsmouth
PAT RICE	Arsenal, Watford
JESSE ROAST	Maidstone United
RON BACON	Norwich City, Gillingham
BOBBY HAM	Bradford PA, Gainsborough Trinity, Grimsby Town, Bradford City, Preston North End, Rotherham United
ALAN LAMB	Preston North End, Port Vale
STEVE GAMMON	Cardiff City
JOHN RELISH	Chester City, Newport County

BELIEVE IT
OR NOT

BIAS NOT SHOWN
Early in 1969 the BBC's Radio 3
'Sports Report' included
coverage of the Chelsea v
Sunderland match at Stamford
Bridge by Mary Raine, a 29-year-
old Sunderland supporter.
Chelsea won 5–1.

DUAL PAYROLL
George Dorling was once
employed by two Football
League clubs at the same time. In
1950–51 he was on the
maintenance staff at Tottenham
Hotspur and was a Gillingham
player.

'Actually, we were robbed'

RED CARD NULLIFIED

On 9 September 1989, Celtic were playing away to St Mirren at Love Street. Tommy Burns had already been booked by the referee when he was shown the red card for dissent as he left the field after being substituted. His replacement Anton Rogan was already on the field, so Celtic completed the remaining three minutes with a full eleven, despite having had a player dismissed.

'VE HAVE VAYS' . . .

Chosen to play for Stoke City against Sheffield United in an FA Cup tie, Stanley Matthews reported sick with influenza. The Stoke management contacted a specialist in the Royal Infirmary for advice. Matthews was given two capsules. They were pep-pills used by Luftwaffe crews on bombing raids over Britain in the Second World War. They worked perfectly. Stoke won 1–0 but at 9 o'clock that night Matthews was so wide awake he could have played another 90 minutes.

THE LONGEST RESULT

In 1988–89 the longest result known in a first-class competition was recorded in the third round of the Welsh Cup: Kidderminster Harriers 3, Llanfair pwllgwyngyllgocerychwyrndrob wllilantysiliogogogoch 0.

CHARLTON'S DAZE

When did Charlton score for Charlton when Charlton could not score? On Easter Saturday 1957, Charlton's goal in a 3–1 Division One defeat was scored by Arsenal defender Stan Charlton when he put through his own goal.

HOME FROM HOME

During the 1920s, Wolverhampton Wanderers had, appropriately in view of their ground's name, a goalkeeper on their books by the name of Richard John Molineux.

SIGN OF THE TIMES

According to a magazine interview in 1990, Vinny Jones (Sheffield United) reads *The Independent* and the *Daily Telegraph*.

GULF WEAR

In January 1991 St Albans City donated their entire first team kit to the Kuwaiti national team.

FLYING DUTCHMAN

Romeo Zondervan, Ipswich Town's Dutch midfield player, holds a private pilot's licence and as a former motor mechanic, restores classic cars as a hobby.

SEASON TO FORGET

In 1989–90, Rangers midfield player Ian Ferguson sustained a back injury at the start of the season then suffered calf, hip, knee, ankle and groin problems followed by a virus infection.

BEYOND BELIEF

On 25 December 1936 in the Wolverhampton Wanderers v Huddersfield Town Division One match at Molineux, Wolves captain Stan Cullis conceded an 86th minute penalty for hands. Bill Hayes scored past goalkeeper Alex Scott. Wolves won 3–1. On 2 October 1937 the same incident occurred again in the corresponding game at Huddersfield in the same minute involving the same three players. This time Huddersfield won 1–0.

EYE OF THE SCORER
Despite losing the sight of one eye at the age of seven in a fireworks accident, Bob Thomson was a more than useful centre-forward. He joined Chelsea from his local club Croydon Common in 1911 and remained until 1922, when he was transferred to Charlton Athletic. Once asked what he did when the ball came on his blind side he replied: 'I close my eye and rely on memory.'

SHORT HISTORY
Alex James' famous baggy shorts were not entirely his own idea. Cartoonist Tom Webster drew him thus clad playing for Preston North End in the *Daily Mail* one Monday, emphasising his small stature. James liked the idea and bought a pair to fit the caricature.

NEEDLE STUCK
In 1947–48 Chesterfield's first 10 points came from away matches and Sunderland had a spell the following season when they took 11 away and none at home.

COLOUR BLIND
In 1895 Arsenal briefly adopted club colours of red and light blue vertical striped shirts.

FANCY MEETING YOU
On 26 January 1991, Burnley and Stockport County met for the 11th time in League and Cup games in exactly 17 months. The breakdown of first class matches was: 4 Division Four, 3 Leyland Daf, 2 FA Cup and 2 Rumbelows Cup games. Between 8 January and 26 January they met three times, the last two encounters within four days when Burnley won successive games 3–2 in the Leyland Daf and Division Four. Burnley won four games, Stockport three and there were four draws.

STUDENT GRANT
When Aston Villa defender Andy Comyn was with Alvechurch, he had arrived from Birmingham University 1st XI in exchange for a bag of kit.

A CHORUS LINE
As a youngster, Jack Jennings was called away from choir practice at his local church to sign for Wigan Borough in the 1930s.

ARSENAL SEE RED
In November 1970 Arsenal carried out tests on their players to determine whether their players were colour blind. They were not.

BLANK VERSE
In Len Shackleton's *Clown Prince of Soccer*, Chapter Nine, page 78, was entitled 'The Average Director's Knowledge of Football'. It was blank.

OXFORD FAILED HONOURS
Ken Oxford played in goal for Manchester City against Arsenal in a Division One game on 24 April 1948 and kept a clean sheet in a 0–0 draw. He was dropped and did not play a first team match for them again before being transferred.

FALLING STARS
When Aston Villa were relegated for the first time in 1935–36, they used 30 different players and 17 of them were either current or future internationals.

MAYBE IT'S BECAUSE . . .
Ned Liddell was a Clapton Orient and Arsenal half-back, manager of Queen's Park Rangers and Fulham, West Ham United assistant manager and chief scout with Chelsea, Brentford and Tottenham Hotspur during his lengthy involvement in the game.

MIST ONCE – MISSED TWICE
On 6 December 1952, Finchley were leading Crystal Palace 3–1 in an FA Cup second round tie when the game was abandoned through fog in the 67th minute. Two Palace forwards had missed the game completely because of being fogbound. The rearranged game produced exactly the same score.

ROLE REVERSING (1)
On 11 April 1936, Fred Sharman played centre-forward in the Leicester City League side at Tottenham. His opposite number for Spurs at centre-half was Doug Hunt. Both players were playing out of their normal positions, to which they returned the following Saturday. Again at Tottenham, Hunt led the Spurs attack while Sharman was at centre-half in this London Combination game.

ROLE REVERSING (2)
In 1948 Bradford Park Avenue were knocked out of the FA Cup by Colchester United. That day Bradford's centre-half was Ron

Greenwood, while his opposite number was Ted Fenton. In 1961 Fenton was succeeded as West Ham United manager by Greenwood.

IT'S A FUNNY OLD GAME
Sam Cowan only took up the game for a joke at the age of 17. He even came in as a late substitute in his first match with just one borrowed boot on. But he subsequently played for Denaby United, Doncaster Rovers and Manchester City, winning an FA Cup winners medal as captain in 1934 and playing for England. Later he joined Bradford City, became a qualified masseur and had successful spells as a manager.

SANDERS OF THE DELIVER
In pre-substitute days, goalkeepers were known to score goals while either suffering from hand injuries or hobbling along in the outfield. But Jim Sanders of West Bromwich Albion once scored direct from a corner kick in a Central League game shortly after the end of the Second World War. Terry Webster was the Derby County reserve goalkeeper beaten by the swerving flag kick.

SITTING IT OUT
John Sitton of Orient was sent off three times during the 1985–86 season. The third time he lasted only two minutes of the game at Burnley.

SHACK SHOCK
On Boxing Day 1954 in a Division One match between Huddersfield Town and Sunderland, the visitors were awarded a corner which was

mildly disputed. The Huddersfield goalkeeper rolled the ball gently in the direction of the corner flag where Sunderland's Len Shackleton was waiting. Before the ball stopped Shackleton hit it back into the goalmouth. The referee ordered him to re-take the corner, but this time Shackleton pushed it over the line for a throw-in.

GOULD FEVER
On 6 January 1975, Bobby Gould was playing for West Ham United at Southampton in an FA Cup third round tie. He was taken off at half-time when it was discovered that he had played for 30 minutes with a broken leg but had managed to head a goal. West Ham won 2–1.

DEFENSIVE OFFENSIVE
Right-half James Lindsay was top scorer for Bury in 1905–06, left-back Jimmy Evans for Southend United in 1921–22 and wing-half Bill Imrie for Newcastle United in 1937–38.

INJECTING STRIFE
After two players of the Uruguayan Division Two club Tanque were suspended in 1990 following positive dope tests, the players union called a strike. The players had taken medicine for colds which the club doctor had prescribed. The suspensions were lifted and the strike called off.

HAMMER B's
In 1963–64 West Ham United might have been tempted to change their nickname to the 'B's. They had twelve players whose surnames began with this letter: Jim Barrett, Peter Bennett, David Bickles, John Bond, Eddie Bovington, Ronnie Boyce, Peter Brabrook, Martin Britt, Ken Brown, Jack Burkett, Dennis Burnett and Johnny Byrne.

CUP REPLACEMENT
The Jules Rimet Trophy, which was the original World Cup, had an unusual history. It spent the war in a shoe box under an Italian official's bed to prevent the Nazis from taking it, was stolen in 1966 and found by a mongrel dog, then presented to Brazil in 1970 after their three wins. But it was stolen again from the headquarters of the Brazilian FA in Rio and probably melted down. The Brazilian branch of a US firm and photographic firm, Kodak Brasileira, offered to provide a duplicate. A goldsmith in Hanau, West Germany, was given the task of manufacturing a copy.

BOMBAY DUCK
In 1938 when a Bombay football team lost by a goal in a local match, their club officials sought a court order declaring the winning goal null and void.

CLOSE ENCOUNTERS
The 20th anniversary season of the Football League in 1908–09 produced the most exciting last six days of any campaign to that date. Apart from Newcastle United clinching the championship and Leicester being relegated, none of the other issues were settled. Bolton Wanderers won the Division Two championship by beating Derby County 1–0 on the last day (30 April) and Liverpool saved themselves from relegation by beating the champions Newcastle by a

similar score on their own ground. Two days earlier Manchester City had lost 1–0 at Bristol City and were relegated on goal average. West Bromwich Albion were similarly denied promotion from Division Two by losing 2–1 to Derby County on 26 April. Early in the season Newcastle had lost 9–1 at home to Sunderland!

TEST MATCH
On 5 March 1991 Lincoln City won 1–0 at Torquay United in a Division Four game. Lincoln goalkeeper Ian Bowling suffered an arm injury in the 52nd minute but carried on. It was only after the game that it was discovered that he had broken it.

NO MISTAKES
A Scottish referee in the 1950s was Charlie Faultless.

FLORIN COIN
The coin used by Referee Mervyn Griffiths, the Welsh referee in the 1953 FA Cup final (Blackpool v Bolton Wanderers), was a two-shilling (10p) piece presented to him by Johnny Farrell, captain of Alloa, after a friendly game with Llanelly at which Griff⁺hs had officiated.

THEY SIKH THEM HERE . . .
In 1967 the first all-Sikh team, complete with turbans, to play in the United Kingdom entered the Bloxwich Combination as Sikh Hunters.

LACKING DOCUMENTARY EVIDENCE
The official programme for the Luton Town v Bristol Rovers

Division Three (South) game on 13 April 1936 did not include the name of Joe Payne. He was the only change from the published teams, coming in at centre-forward for Boyd. He scored ten goals in the 12–0 win. John Ellis the Rovers goalkeeper kept his place in the side for the rest of the season.

PUTTING THE BOOT IN
During Leeds United's League Cup semi-final first leg game at Derby County in 1967–68, United defender Paul Madeley lost one boot in the Baseball Ground mud and played on without it until the ball went dead. It was only after a lengthy search that the missing footwear was discovered.

PRE-WAR INVENTION?
An item in a 1937 newspaper reported: 'Gillingham yesterday transferred a forward to Aston Villa in exchange for three second-hand turnstiles, a typewriter, two goalkeepers' sweaters, an assistant trainer and three jars of weedkiller.' No names were given.

OVERALL QUALITY
On 28 February 1925 Cardiff City beat Newcastle United 3–0 in a Division One match despite the fact that seven of their players were on international duty the same day.

WINS OF WAR
Everton won the League Championship in the season before the competition was stopped because of the First World War (1914–15) and again in 1938–39 prior to the Second World War.

GAMES OF ONE HALF

Len Dutton was a pre-Second World War Arsenal amateur. He played in several friendlies and one competitive game at left-half for the 'A' team in the Southern League against Norwich City on Good Friday 1939. Norwich won 4–0. On 12 January 1952 in an FA Cup third round tie, he was at right-half for Norwich when they lost 5–0 to Arsenal.

DILLY-ALLY CRILLEY

In 1921–22 Wee Willie Crilley – all 5ft 1in – scored 49 of Alloa's 81 League goals in Division Two. In one game against King's Park at Forthbank, Stirling, he managed to wriggle through the legs of the opposing centre-half and with only the goalkeeper to beat invited the visiting fans behind the goal to decide which side of the goal to put the ball. He obliged.

LEAVING IT LATE

In 1958–59 Dunfermline Athletic appeared certain for relegation from Division One before the last game of the season. But they beat Partick Thistle 10–1 with winger Harry Melrose scoring six goals for a post-war Scottish record.

FLEETING CATFORD

Charlton Athletic played one season at The Mount, Catford, in 1923–24. The ground was the home of Catford Southend FC, an amateur club in the London League. The two clubs amalgamated and Charlton attempted to change its name to the existing one but were refused permission by the Football League. Disgruntled supporters formed their own amateur club called Old Charlton, applied to take Catford Southend's London League place and were accepted.

The first game at The Mount was not played until 22 December against Northampton Town before a crowd of 8000. Charlton wore Catford's dark and light blue stripes. But the move was a total disaster. An FA Cup tie had to be switched to The Valley and facilities and attendances were so poor that Charlton returned there at the end of the season. Catford Southend were re-formed and played in the Kent League, but were wound up after one season themselves.

TALENTED RESERVES

On 27 February 1954, Berwick Rangers beat Dundee from Division One 3–0 in the Scottish Cup third round to reach the quarter-finals. Berwick at the time were in Division 'C' and had finished their fixtures in sixth place. Runners-up in their League were Dundee Reserves.

BARE FACTS

On 25 February 1991, Nottingham Forest substitute Nigel Jemson was called upon to replace the injured Steve Hodge in a fifth round FA Cup tie at Southampton. As he peeled off his tracksuit top he discovered that he had left his shirt in the dressing-room. He had to use the shirt of the other substitute Ian Woan. Ruel Fox did the same when trying to replace Lee Power for Norwich City against Coventry City in Division One on 6 April 1991.

BACK TO EARTH

When Mo Johnston missed an easy scoring chance for Rangers at Aberdeen on 2 March 1991 he picked up a piece of mud and threw it to the ground in annoyance. In doing so he ricked his back and missed the next game.

TIME WARP (2)
In November 1955 a game between 415 Coast Regiment and 46 AA Regiment at Gravesend produced a first half lasting 70 minutes when the referee's watch stopped. Coast Regiment eventually won 4–2.

LISTED BUILDINGS
After Wolverhampton Wanderers won their FA Cup semi-final in 1893, a local builder constructed a row of houses and put a miniature of the Cup on each front gate. When Wolves went on to win the trophy itself he built another row with the houses named after the players in the team.

LOOKING BACK IN ANGER
On 1 March 1975 in the Division Two game between Sunderland and West Bromwich Albion at Roker Park, Albion goalkeeper John Osborne was injured but carried on until a penalty was awarded against his team. He handed the goalkeeper's jersey to Gordon Nisbet, whose first two senior games for Albion had actually been in goal. But Tony Towers hit the post with his penalty attempt. Osborne returned to goal but conceded three goals.

OLDEST SWINGER IN TOWN
Sam Phillips was banned from attending Ledbury Town's home matches during 1980–81 for allegedly assaulting a referee. He had apparently rendered the referee's shirt 'torn beyond repair'. But he still watched his team through a gap in the hedge surrounding the ground. Phillips was variously described as aged between 77 and 82.

RARE ROVERS RETURN
On 4 January 1982, Thurlestone Rovers from South Devon earned their first League point in two years, drawing 3–3 with Centrax.

MODEST EXPOSURE
On 10 February 1979, the day after Nottingham Forest signed Trevor Francis for £1 million, he played for the 'A' team at Notts County in front of a crowd of 40. Afterwards the FA said he was not properly registered and the Football League said they had not received the player's registration.

KEW'S QUEUE
In 1972–73 Football League referee Gordon Kew set up a record by dismissing seven players in the competition during the season.

RIGGING THE RESULT
During the League South game between West Bromwich Albion and Southampton on 24 November 1945 at the Hawthorns, Albion left-winger Arthur Rowley dashed in to head a centre, missed the ball and finished in the back of the net clutching the rigging which collapsed on top of him. One goalpost had snapped at its base. Temporary repairs were carried out and the remaining few minutes of the match were completed though Southampton, losing 5–2, wanted it abandoned.

'Now you know what a fish feels like'

BLOCK BOOKING

Referee Peter Willis booked eight players in the Doncaster Rovers v Hereford United match in 1979–80, including seven Hereford players in one incident when their defensive wall refused to retreat 10 yards at a free-kick.

SAVING GRACE

On 7 April 1980, Arsenal included six reserves against Tottenham Hotspur, resting their star players for the European Cup-Winners Cup semi-final with Juventus. The Gunners still won 2–1.

MOTORING IN MIDFIELD

Austin Morris was a left-half with Mansfield Town in pre-war days.

BORDERLINE CASES

Grenville Jones was born in Nuneaton of Welsh parents. He won England schoolboy honours and joined Wrexham from West Bromwich Albion in 1955. The family lived in Saltney on one side of the road in Wales. The other side was in England. Bobby Evans was actually born in Saltney. A left-winger with Wrexham, he had played ten times for Wales after the turn of the century when it was discovered he had been born on the English side of the road. They also capped him. But there was no problem for Saltney based left-winger David Jones in 1956. He had been born in a nursing home in Chester.

FITNESS FREAKS

South African goalkeeper Ken Hewkins, who joined Fulham from Clyde, had injury problems in 1959–60. Playing his way back to fitness in the reserves he had the misfortune to let in eight goals against Aldershot and then in a match with Gillingham was given the task of taking a penalty. He had his kick saved and the Kent club were able to score at the other end before he could regain his position.

RUGG ON THE CARPET

At the end of the match between Montrose and Berwick Rangers on 2 January 1960, John Rugg the Berwick centre-half was attacked by a spectator. There had been no trouble during the match which Montrose had won 2–1.

FUNNY FINNEYS

Although Alan Finney spent 16 years with Sheffield Wednesday as an outside-right until he joined Doncaster Rovers in January 1966, his brother Brian was attached to clubs in all divisions during a six-month spell in 1958: Sheffield Wednesday (Division Two), Manchester United (Division One), Carlisle United (Division Four) and Doncaster Rovers (Division Three). He then went to Scarborough.

NICE SINKING FEELING

Bill Wainscoat, a former Leeds United player, was given an oil well in Canada for scoring a brilliant goal on tour there before the Second World War.

BIG CHIEF PLANT'EM

Jimmy Seed, manager of Charlton Athletic's team in their 1939 tour of Canada, was made a Red Indian Chief by the Sioux. He was even given a head-dress.

SHORT TYPE LONG

When Harold Williams was at school, his teacher was not keen on him playing football, fearful of him being hurt because of his size. But at 5ft 4in he turned professional with Leeds United, playing 228 League and Cup games and was capped for Wales as a right-winger.

HUNGARIAN MIST ENGLAND MISSED

Before playing England at Wembley in 1953, the Hungarians trained in special fog surroundings. At Lake Bulaton they had a machine emanating a chemical substance which simulated fog. It proved unnecessary. Hungary had a clear cut 6–3 win.

CHOC-HOLIC?

Reg Baines was a goalscoring centre-forward between the wars. In the mid-1920s he played for York City in the Midland League. Subsequently he played for Selby Town, Scarborough, Barnsley, York again, Sheffield United, Doncaster Rovers and Halifax Town to complete his Yorkshire circuit as he did not want to leave his job in a York chocolate factory.

POSITIONAL CHANGES

In October 1957 Billy Myerscough played for Aston Villa in Division One, occupying in five consecutive matches the outside-left, centre-forward, outside-right, inside-left and inside-right position.

THROW-IN GOAL

Frank Bokas scored with a throw-in for Barnsley against Manchester United on 22 January 1938 in an FA Cup fourth round tie. United goalkeeper Tommy Breen touched the ball as it went over his head.

PUNCH BALL

Peter McBride, the Preston North End and Scottish goalkeeper, once punched a cross-shot from Billy Meredith, the ball bouncing twice before landing in the arms of the goalkeeper at the opposite end.

BEACHED WAIL

In May 1974, Brian Doyle, the manager of Stockport County, complained that he had been sacked because he lived in Blackpool, 60 miles away.

KILLIE CRANKIES?

Stranraer players train twice a week at Kilmarnock, 60 miles from the ground.

QUICK KICK FIX

On 20 October 1973 Charlton Athletic were playing Rochdale in a Division Three match. Charlton were awarded a goal-kick, but as referee Derek Civil and one of his linesmen walked away towards the middle of the pitch, goalkeeper John Dunn pushed the ball out to defender Ray Tumbridge from the edge of the penalty area, not the goal area. Colin Powell carried on the move and from his cross Arthur Horsfield scored. The goal was allowed to stand. Charlton won 3–0.

ADVERTISING PLEA

In November 1983 during an injury crisis at Watford, the club placed this advert in *The Times*: 'Wanted: Professional footballers men (or women) aged 18–80 preference given to applicants with two arms and two legs in working order.'

SIMPLE SUMS

In 1952–53 Berwick Rangers left-half was Ronnie Mitchell, a BSc, PhD and lecturer in mathematics at St Andrews.

JUBILEE STAMPED

In their silver jubilee season 1960–61, Ipswich Town won the Division Two championship. But they crashed to their heaviest defeat in the Cup, losing 7–1 at Southampton. They were six down at half-time, the Saints having scored four goals in seven minutes. George O'Brien hit a hat-trick in 28 minutes.

THE WHISKY-MAC DONS

Before Aberdeen's 1937 Scottish Cup tie against Inverness Thistle, trainer Donal Colman used whisky to massage the stiff muscles of his players on a freezing afternoon. Many of the team wore gloves. Goalkeeper George Johnstone had particular difficulty in keeping warm as Aberdeen had an easy 6–0 win over the Highland League club.

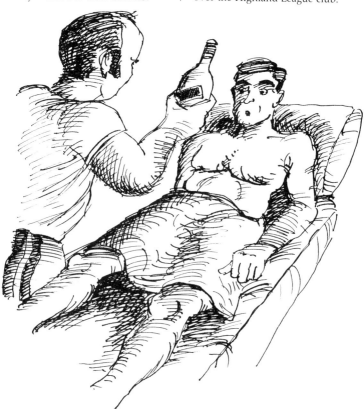

'Now the game's over, can't you spare a wee dram?'

GOOD NEWS . . .
AND BAD

ERRATIC BEHAVIOUR
In 1968–69 Rochdale fans were awarded a £100 prize as the best behaved spectators in Division Four. A few days later the FA ordered the club to post warning notices on the ground after some of them had thrown objects onto the pitch.

ST PETER'S AND OTHERS DEMISE
On 17 November 1923, Hartlepools United met unbeaten St Peter's Albion, members of the Tyneside League, in the FA Cup. Hartlepools led 8–0 at half-time, Billy Smith the centre-forward having scored five including a penalty. Smith added two more goals in the second half in a 10–1 win. But against Walsall in January, Smith was sent off and at the end of the season the team finished second from bottom on goal average, their worst position since being formed.

SHIP TO SURE
In the 1938–39 Scottish Cup, Celtic began their involvement by being drawn away to Burntisland Shipyard in the first round and conceded three goals. This is the highest number of goals they had ever let in against an amateur side. But they did score eight themselves.

PUDDEFOOT IN HIS MOUTH?
Syd Puddefoot was signed by Falkirk from West Ham United in February 1922 for a then record fee of £6000. Most of the fee was raised by supporters and the player was paraded through the town accompanied by a pipe-band. Although he had guested for the club during the war and impressed, his official debut was in the Scottish Cup against Bathgate. Falkirk lost 1–0.

BELL'S CLANGER
In 1890–91 Celtic fielded an ineligible player named Bell in two matches. They won both, but subsequently had the points deducted.

AN ILL WIND
Arthur Gale played in every round of West Bromwich Albion's 1934–35 FA Cup run up to the final, scoring in the first four games. He had been deputy for the injured Tommy Glidden. But Glidden was brought back for the final against Sheffield Wednesday, only to break down injured as Albion lost 4–2.

BEAM ME UP . . .
Roy Kirk was playing for Coventry City at Northampton Town on 20 November 1954 in an FA Cup tie. He hit a long upfield pass, but the ball bounced over goalkeeper Alf Wood's head and into the net from 80 yards. On another occasion when he was playing for Leeds United in a Central League game against Preston North End, Leeds were leading

1–0. They were awarded a penalty, but Kirk shot wide. They were given another spot kick. He hit it at the goalkeeper, but when the penalty was again retaken, he scored. In 1954–55 against Huddersfield Town in an FA Cup third round replay at Coventry, he hit an upright from a penalty. On 20 September 1954 in another Coventry game, against Leyton Orient, he put through his own goal twice in a 2–2 draw.

SNOW RESCUE
On 15 January 1955, the Hibernian v Queen of the South Division One match was the only one to escape frozen and snowbound grounds. But even this was abandoned after 70 minutes with Hibs leading 3–0, as one goal-line had become obscured by the snow. Bobby Johnstone had scored all three Hibs goals. The replayed fixture on 16 April 1955 was drawn 1–1 and the point helped 'Queens' to avoid relegation.

THE LATE, LATE LOW
On 5 January 1971 Huddersfield Town won 2–0 at Birmingham. In the closing minutes of the game, Huddersfield goalkeeper

Terry Poole was carried off with a broken leg. Winger Steve Smith went in goal and broke his thumb.

REPEATING WOLVES
Playing at Leeds on 12 December 1936, Wolverhampton Wanderers lost centre-half Stan Cullis with a broken collar bone and had goalkeeper Alex Scott sent off. The match was abandoned in fog with seven minutes remaining and Wolves leading. The replay on 21 April saw Wolves win 1–0 again.

MEMORABLE START
On 25 August 1990, Sean McCarthy made his debut for Bradford City against Tranmere Rovers in Division Three. He missed a penalty kick, scored a goal and was later sent off for two bookable offences. Bradford lost 2–1.

HORNE'S ON A DILEMMA
On 25 August 1990 John Horne, 18, made his debut for Hamilton Academical at Falkirk. He scored after seven minutes but was dismissed in the 49th.

ON HIS TODD
On 22 September 1990 Kevin Todd, making his initial appearance after being signed from Whitley Bay, scored a hat-trick for Berwick Rangers at East Stirling in Division Two, hit the woodwork twice and was booked during a 4–0 win.

DELAYED REACTION
On 10 November 1990, Maidstone United were awarded their first penalty kick in 13 months in a Division Four match with Hereford United. Gary Cooper scored from it, but missed another in the 1–1 draw.

FRESH FIELDS
In 1959–60 Malcolm Newlands, playing in goal for Workington reserves against Doncaster Rovers reserves, was injured and forced to play on the right wing. He scored a hat-trick, including one penalty.

DEAD BALL REVIVAL
On 25 November 1972 during the Bolton Wanderers v Rotherham United game, Rotherham goalkeeper Jim McDonagh thought the ball had gone out of play and placed it for a goal-kick. But Garry Jones nipped in and pushed the ball into the net for what was the winning goal, 2–1 to Bolton.

UNFAIR TO JACK
Jack Fairbrother kept goal in three FA Cup ties in successive seasons on Charlton Athletic's ground at The Valley. With Preston North End he appeared in 1946 and 1947 and again with Newcastle United in 1948. He let in six in a 1949 replay and two in each of the following two appearances, finishing on the losing side three times.

TOUCH OF MAGIC
Steve Kirk came on as a substitute in the 78th minute for Motherwell at Aberdeen on 26 January 1991 in a Scottish Cup third round tie at Pittodrie. He scored the only goal of the game with his first touch and was then booked for overdoing the celebrations.

TRAVELLERS FARE

Aston Villa were returning by
train from a pre-season friendly
in Scotland on a hot August day
in the early post-war era. The
players were feeling parched.
Harry Parkes volunteered to
dash into the refreshment room
at Preston Station, grab a tray of
14 teas and climb aboard again.
As the train slowed down, he
leapt off and vanished in the
direction of the station buffet.
Unfortunately the train did not
stop and continued slowly on its
journey without him.

RELEGATION BLUES

Cardiff City conceded only 59
goals in 1928–29, the smallest
total in Division One.
Manchester City scored the

highest number with 80 goals in 1937–38. But both teams were relegated.

MIDGET MINDED

Midget Moffat was a 5ft Workington winger. Arsenal offered him terms in May 1923 but he travelled to Woolwich, thinking the club was still playing there. He was taken on the club's Scandinavian tour to Denmark, Sweden and Norway and played in all seven games on the right wing. But Arsenal chairman Henry Norris had a cast iron rule that no player under 5ft 8 inches or weighing less than 11 stone would be signed. So Moffat moved to Luton Town, then Everton and Oldham Athletic.

OVERSHADOWING EVENT

Peter Shilton made his 900th League appearance on 25 August 1990 for Derby County at Chelsea. In the last minute of the game, Chelsea's goalkeeper Dave Beasant saved a penalty kick from Dean Saunders and Derby lost 2–1.

'Come back when you've grown up'

EYEING FOR NELSON

Fred Laycock, playing at inside-right for Barrow against Rotherham United on 16 March 1925, the transfer deadline day, was called off the field to sign for Nelson.

LEFT BANKS

Shortly after Gordon Banks, later of England fame, was selected to play for Sheffield Boys, he was dropped because of poor performance in a Yorkshire Schools Cup tie.

WHAT'S IN A NAME

FORESTATION
Four cul-de-sacs on a new housing estate in Nottingham have been named Clough Court, Chapman Court, Pearce Court and Gaynor Court. Lee Chapman has since left Forest for Leeds.

GETTING LONGER
Measured performances could have been expected from these players: Eddie Inch, an Irish wing-half in the mid-1930's; Bobby Foot (Southend United) in the 1950s; and Ernie Yard (Bury) and Terry Miles (Port Vale) in the 1960s.

SHANKLY MOVED ON
In 1953 Bradford Park Avenue drew up a short list of two from applicants for their vacant manager's job. They decided on Norman Kirkman. The unlucky candidate was Bill Shankly. Kirkman quit in 1954 and in the next five years became a baker, estate agent, aircraft worker, insurance representative and travelling salesman.

STUNG LIKE A BEE
In 1961 India's outstanding player was Mohamed Ali, a 23-year-old wing half from Calicutt FC in the Calcutta Football League and nicknamed 'The Bengal Lancer'.

FIVE ASSORTED THROSTLES
In 1957–58 West Bromwich Albion had five unrelated Williams on their books: Stuart, Graham, Mark, David and Geoff.

DOUBLE DUTCH
The name of a Dutchman who played in goal for both Arsenal and Charlton Athletic in the 1930s caused endless confusion. An amateur, he combined playing with his job as a wholesale fruiterer. At Highbury he played in the first 12 games of Arsenal's 1930–31 League Championship winning season and was known as Gerrie Keyser. The following season he played 17 times for Charlton in Division Two and was called Piet Keizer.

BALL AT THE DOUBLE
In 1963–64 Blackpool had two unrelated players called Ball. Alan had been an apprentice in September 1961 and turned professional in May 1962. Allan signed amateur forms in August 1963 but had his registration cancelled four months later.

LONDON PRIDE
In 1959 the directors of Charlton Athletic considered changing the name of the club to London Athletic FC but decided against it.

JACK AND GYM
A H Gibbons, an England amateur international forward who played for Brentford and Tottenham Hotspur before turning professional with Bradford Park Avenue and returning later to Brentford, had a career which spanned the Second World War. His first names were Albert Henry, but he was always known as Jack to avoid confusion with Bert,

Bertie, Albert and Herbert who were fellow members at a boys' gym. Even the family adopted the nickname.

COMMON GROUND
In 1954–55 Torquay United had two Jack Smiths, one a full-back signed from Plymouth Argyle, another a left-winger from Liverpool. In addition they had another full-back called Harry Smith.

BRIGHT SPARK
Hyam Dimmer was a Scotstoun born inside-right who developed with Western Men's Own Church and Kilsyth Rangers before turning professional with Ayr United in pre-war days. In August 1946 he joined Aldershot having assisted them as a guest player for the reserves the previous season.

APTLY NAMED
Allenby Chilton, Manchester United centre-half from 1938, took his first name from the Field Marshal in the First World War. In the Second World War, Chilton landed at Normandy on D-Day with the Durham Light Infantry and was wounded at Caen.

WHEN BLACKADDER WENT NORTH
Fred Blackadder was a centre-half who joined Carlisle United as an amateur before the Second World War, having previously been with Queen's Park. He entered the RAF, became a Physical Training Instructor and in 1940–41 guested for Bournemouth. He also played in RAF representative teams at home and abroad and made one

peacetime Football League appearance in 1946–47 for Carlisle in Division Three (North).

MODERN TIMES
Between the wars, Wolverhampton Wanderers had a goalkeeper on their books by the name of Charlie Chaplin. He did not break into their senior side but made occasional outings in the Central League team.

NO LEFT-WING TORY
In 1956–57 Winston Churchill played two games as an amateur for Chelsea in their Hornchurch and District League side at outside-left.

. . . MORE PRIME MINISTERIAL REMINDERS
In the late 1950s there was a half-back with Aston Villa and Walsall called Anthony Eden, while Neville Chamberlain, a forward, played for a variety of clubs in the 1980s including Port Vale and Stoke City.

SCOUTS SELECTION?
Darlington had an outside-right in the 1950s called Baden Powell.

COMEDIANS
Bob Hope was an inside-forward with West Bromwich Albion, Birmingham City and Sheffield Wednesday.

IAN TIMES TWO
In September 1987 Brechin City

signed Ian A Paterson, a centre-forward from Montrose. In December 1988 they secured Ian G Paterson a defender from Glenrothes Juniors.

TAYLORS MADE AGAIN
East Fife signed Paul H Taylor, a centre-back from Sauchie Juniors, and Paul Taylor, a left-back from Whitburn Juniors, in the 1989–90 season. In pre-war days Bolton Wanderers had a George Taylor and a George T Taylor.

HAMMER HOUSE
On 2 September 1972, streets in the London Borough of Newham were named after Bobby Moore and Trevor Brooking.

ONE IN (PAST) A MILLION
Esmond Million made a

No ball games here?

successful debut at 18 for Middlesbrough against Port Vale on 6 October 1956 despite conceding a goal. Middlesbrough won 3–1.

TWO-SEATER MORRIS

In 1930–31, Crewe Alexandra had a right-half called Harold Morris and an inside-right called Harry Morris.

THE MOST EXPENSIVE TEAM?

Over the last 60 years this might be thought to have been the most expensive Football League side:

BILLY GOLD . . . . Bournemouth, Wolverhampton Wanderers, Chelsea and Doncaster Rovers

BILLY BONDS . . . . Charlton Athletic and West Ham United

KEVIN NOTEMAN . . . . . Leeds United and Doncaster Rovers

PETER COYNE . . . . Manchester United, Crewe Alexandra, Swindon Town and Aldershot

RICHARD MONEY . . . . . . Scunthorpe United, Fulham, Liverpool, Luton Town, Portsmouth and Scunthorpe United

STUART CASH . . . . Nottingham Forest

LEN RICH . . . . Plymouth Argyle

PAUL JEWELL . . . . Liverpool, Wigan Athletic and Bradford City

TONY DIAMOND . . . . . . Blackburn Rovers and Blackpool

DAVID CROWN . . . . Brentford, Portsmouth, Reading, Southend United and Gillingham

WORRELL STERLING . . . Watford and Peterborough United

Substitutes:

KEN POUND . . . . Swansea City, Bournemouth and Gillingham

SHAUN PENNY . . . . Bristol City and Bristol Rovers

THE NUMBERS GAME

HOME SWINGS
Millwall scored 87 goals in home matches in Division Three (South) in 1927–28 while Arsenal scored only 11 in Division One during 1912–13 during their home programme. In 1925–26 Barrow lost 15 of their 21 home League games.

FIGURE IT OUT
A football team can be changed in 39916800 ways always using the same 11 players – simply multiply 1 x 2 x 3 x 4 x 5 x 6 x 7 x 8 x 9 x 10 x 11.

MOORE THE MERRIER?
When West Germany beat England 2–1 in a Youth international match at Bolton on 12 March 1958, their inside-right Conrad Heidner was the outstanding player, scoring both goals. Perhaps his elusiveness could have been attributed to the fact that in the first half he wore a number 10 shirt and a number 13 one in the second half. His immediate opponent was Bobby Moore.

STILL ON NINE
Frank Haffey of Celtic was the goalkeeper on the receiving end when England beat Scotland 9–3 at Wembley in 1961. On 26 October 1963 he was playing for Celtic against Airdrieonians in a Division One game. With the score 9–0 he was asked to take a penalty, but his shot was brilliantly saved by 18-year-old Roddy McKenzie.

SHORT AND THE LONG
Will Buchan was 5ft 6in and the elder of four brothers; Charlie had a 20-year career in the game and became a celebrated international playing for Sunderland and Arsenal, Tom was a utility player for Bolton Wanderers winning representative honours while Jack was a professional whose career was terminated with injury at Charlton Athletic. All three were around 6ft tall.

LITTLE AND GOOD
Some of the shortest players to appear for England have been: goalkeeper Teddy Davison (Sheffield Wednesday) 5ft 7in, full-back Herbert Burgess (Manchester City) 5ft 5in, half-back Tommy Magee (West Bromwich Albion) 5ft 3in and forward Fanny Walden (Tottenham Hotspur) 5ft 2¾ in.

DRAWN THEORY ONLY
Darwen won 14 and lost 16 of 30 Division Two matches in the 1896–97 season.

WELSH VOTES WASTED
No club which never played in the Football League received more votes when applying for membership than Llanelly's 25 in 1932.

UNRELATED HEIGHTS
In 1953–54, Tipton born defender Roy Oakley, who had

been signed from Channel Islands football, was the tallest player on Southampton's staff at 6ft 2½ in. Unrelated local born right-winger Derek Oakley was the shortest at 5ft 5¾in.

CHARLES THE FOURTH

Charlie Ashcroft made his Football League debut for Liverpool against Chelsea at Anfield on 7 September 1946. He was beaten four times but Liverpool scored seven goals. Four days later he conceded five against Manchester United but Liverpool failed to score once.

ARITHMETICAL DEPRESSION

Peter Desmond played in twice as many international games as he did Division One matches. Signed by Middlesbrough from Shelbourne in 1949 he was included at inside-left in the Republic of Ireland team which defeated England 2–0 at Goodison Park on 21 September 1949. Only five years later he was playing in the North-Eastern League for Blackhall Colliery Welfare having been with eight clubs since leaving Middlesbrough in May 1950. At Ayresome Park he made only two League appearances before moving to Southport where he scored twice in 12 games. He subsequently played for Fleetwood, York City (one League game), Stockton, Wisbech, Spalding, Hartlepool United (one League game) and then Blackhall. He was capped four times during 1949–50.

MINI-MARATHON MAN

Referee R W Blake, equipped with a pedometer, officiated at a Liverpool v Blackpool Division One match in 1938. In the first half he covered 3 miles 1520 yards, in the second half 2 miles 960 yards. Total: 6 miles 720 yards.

POSITIONAL CHANGES

Eric Hayward had a 20-year career spanning the Second World War era, as a centre-half playing for Port Vale and Blackpool without scoring a goal. Neil Franklin did the same over 17 years before his first goal for Crewe Alexandra in March 1956. Yet Steve Bruce managed his 11th League goal of the season for Manchester United in 1990–91 on 30 March to become the highest scoring player in that position in one Football League season. His final total for the season was 13.

SEEING YELLOW AND GREEN

In 1973–74 Peter Millar of Motherwell was booked five times in as many League and Cup games against Celtic.

DISAPPEARING YOUTH

In 1990–91 only five of the 15-strong Liverpool youth team which had taken part in an Easter tournament in Italy in February 1986 were still playing in the Football League. Alex Watson was transferred to Bournemouth from Anfield, while Jim Magilton had gone to Oxford United. Terry McPhillips started the season on Halifax's books and John Jeffers was with Port Vale. Only Wayne Harrison remained at Liverpool.

JOB SECURITY

In 1984 Milos Milutinovic became Yugoslavia's 28th different national coach in 38 years.

GALLUP TO THE WORLD CUP
A Gallup poll taken before the USA was awarded the 1994 World Cup revealed that 49 percent of adults expressed an interest in visiting a game in the tournament if it was held there.

NEVER SAY EVER AGAIN
In 1991 Ever Almeida, a Uruguayan by birth and the Olimpia (Paraguay) goalkeeper, retired at 43. He finished his career by helping his club to a double: the South American Cup and the South American Super Cup.

STIRLING BALANCE
In 1963–64 Stirling Albion finished bottom of Division Two and used 50 different players during the season. In 1964–65 they were champions and promoted to Division One.

COUNTER ATTRACTIONS
When Everton and Liverpool met in the FA Cup semi-final at Villa Park on 31 March 1906, Everton won 2–0 in front of a crowd of around 50000. Despite the fact that it was also Grand National Day at Aintree, at Anfield some 15000 saw Liverpool reserves beat their neighbours 4–2 in a Lancashire Combination Division One derby, while at Goodison Park a sprinkling of spectators saw Balmoral and Southport Trinity in the final of the Liverpool Amateur Cup.

WARTIME RESTRICTIONS
Celtic did not come out very well during Second World War matches with Rangers. In 1940–41 they won 3–2 at Ibrox and 1–0 there in 1943–44 and 1944–45. But in seven seasons of wartime and transitional fare Celtic did not win an Old Firm League match at Parkhead.

FROZEN ASSETS
The harsh winter of 1946–47 produced many postponements and some low attendances. When Bolton Wanderers met Leeds United on 3 February 1947 in a Division One game the crowd was only 4280.

ERIC THE TWELFTH
Trick question: who was the first player to wear a number 12 jersey in an FA Cup Final? The answer: Eric Brook, outside-left of Manchester City in the 1933 final against Everton when the teams were numbered from 1 to 22.

ST GEORGE AND THE DRAG-ON
Bristol St George in the Gloucester County League drew their opening nine games in 1986–87, eight of them by 1–1. The sequence was broken on 27 September when they lost 1–0 at home to Elwood.

NO CON MAN
Con Martin made 213 League and FA Cup appearances for Aston Villa between 1948 and 1956. Of these 176 were at centre-half, eight at right-back, two at left-back and 27 as goalkeeper.

LOCAL EVENT
On 25 March 1975 Notts County played their 3000th League game. It was a 2–2 draw with Nottingham Forest.

THE FAMOUS FIVE

In an Eastern Counties League game in November 1950 at Clacton's Old Road ground, referee EH Morrison awarded Tottenham Hotspur 'A' team a penalty. The kick was taken five times before the official was satisfied that the goalkeeper had not moved.

Take one! George Ludford shot at goalkeeper Ken Starling who punched the ball out.

Take two! Ludford shot over the bar.

Take three! Ludford's shot was again punched away by Starling.

Take four! Groundstaff boy Higgins scored.

Take five! Higgins scored again. The referee was satisfied, but the game was abandoned in fog with Spurs leading 4–1.

Seven weeks later in January, Lowestoft right-half Peter Moody had five attempts from a penalty against Newmarket Town. Three times the referee ordered the kick to be retaken because Lowestoft players moved into the area. The fourth time a Newmarket player encroached, and the fifth saw Moody's shot saved by the opposing goalkeeper.

'Ready when you are, Mr de Mille'

VICTORIA MILESTONE

On 15 March 1971, Hartlepool United entertained Brentford at the Victoria Ground and drew 0–0. It was the one-millionth League game to have been played since the inception of the Football League in 1888.

FOLLOW THAT ACT

Burnley goalkeeper Jerry Dawson was with the club from 1906 to 1929 and made 522 Football League appearances. During this time he had 47 different understudies. On one windy day at Turf Moor he took a goal-kick and it blew off for a corner.

COUPON BUSTERS (1)

All home teams won in Division One on 23 February 1926, Division Three (South) on 3 April 1926 and Division Three (North) on 14 March 1931. Nine of the 11 Division One games on 18 September 1948 were drawn but on Christmas Day 1937 none of the home teams won in Division Three (North).

COUPON BUSTERS (2)

There was only one home win in Division Two on 7 May 1921, in Division Two on 15 October 1921, in Division One on 25 November 1922 and in Division Two on 27 August 1927. On 10 December 1955 all home teams in Division One won their matches.

ROOM AT THE TOP

On 28 April 1923 only ten goals were scored in ten Division One matches.

LONDON LINKS

On 13 February 1937 none of London's eleven Football League clubs lost, but on 22 December 1951 not one of them managed to win.

SOCCER AND SHOW BUSINESS

WELL BALANCED
Radio and TV personality 'Diddy' David Hamilton, a self-confessed Fulham supporter, contributed to football magazine *Soccer Star* during the 1950s under his previous name David Pilditch. More recently he described himself as 'centre-forward for Subbuteo'.

CELLULOID HERO
In 1920, Arsenal centre-forward Harold Walden was the hero in football's first film, *The Winning Goal*. Yet he played only two League games for the club, scoring in the second of these against Oldham Athletic in the 1920–21 season.

RAY'S A LAUGH
Comedian Ted Ray was once on the books of Liverpool and played for their third team.

GRACIE AND FAVOUR
Rochdale pre-war singing personality Gracie Fields kicked off in a Preston North End pre-season trial match for charity on 16 August 1934. Proceeds from the game went to the local Royal Infirmary.

CABARET PERFORMERS
Pat Liney, a goalkeeper who played for both Bradford City and Bradford Park Avenue, was often seen on cabaret circuit as a singer. Park Avenue had an amateur Roy Hedges who was better known as nightclub artist Dean Raymond.

CROWING
Jack Cock was the first Cornishman to be capped for England in 1920. He later became a popular variety star and possessed a fine tenor voice, appearing in most of the leading theatres. In 1930 he was even signed up to appear in a film.

NO COACHES PLEASE
A 1950s cartoon film in Russia called *An Extraordinary Match* depicted two teams, one full of energy, working like robots, the other better organised and playing intelligently. Brains won over brawn.

TWO-TIERED OZON LAYER
In 1957 the first night of an opera in Bucharest called 'Bujor XII' had to be cancelled. The leading man Titus Ozon was an international footballer with the Romanian side and away on tour.

HOLLYWOOD SUCCESS
Neil Paterson played for Dundee United as an amateur while employed as a journalist with the local DC Thomson group of newspapers. In 1936–37 he made 25 League appearances, scoring nine goals, and captained the team in the second half of the season. The following season he

made one appearance before moving to London at the age of 22 and did not play first-class football again. A freelance journalist and writer, several of his books and stories were made into feature films and he also worked on documentary films. In the late 1950s as a screenplay writer he went to Hollywood where he later won an Oscar for his screenplay *Room at the Top* in 1960.

DRESS CIRCLE

Alf Ramsay was the only Tottenham Hotspur player in the England squad in 1953. The party were taken to a West End cinema as part of their social function. There was some amusement and not a little ribbing when it was revealed that the film was *The Naked Spur*. But it turned out to be a Western starring James Stewart and Janet Leigh.

Double feature but not much exposure

HOWLERS

MEDAL FATIGUE
In 1914 the FA Cup medals bore the words English Cup not FA Cup, due to an error.

'TAKE HIS NAME'(X 200)
A match involving the Royal Horse Artillery in Palestine in the late 1940s was refereed by a sergeant-major. Barracked so much, he stopped the game and ordered a sergeant to take the names of every man standing between the half-way line and one of the goalposts.

DOWNWARD CAREER MOVE
Raith Rovers goalkeeper Jim Thorburn let in more than 100 goals in 1962–63 as his club was relegated to Division Two. He moved to Ipswich Town. They were relegated at the end of the next season.

NIFTY SAM
Tottenham Hotspur's White Hart Lane ground was the stage for an unusual corner-kick. On 12 April 1924 Everton were the visitors in a Division One match. Their right-winger Sam Chedgzoy decided to expose a loophole in the laws which then allowed for the kicker to play the ball more than once without it touching another player. He dribbled the ball along the line and scored. After this episode the law was suitably amended.

LONG FISHY TALE
Frank Whiting, a pre-First World War goalkeeper for Brighton & Hove Albion, could kick a football from one goal to over the crossbar at the other end.

DES DOES IT
Daily Express columnist Desmond Hackett said that he would jump in the lake near his hotel if England failed to beat Belgium in the 1954 World Cup. They drew 4–4 and he kept his promise.

MISSING FILM
Copies of the 16mm sound film of the 1960 European Cup Final between Real Madrid and Eintracht Frankfurt were sold by the BBC Film Library at a cost of £35. The film ran for 85 minutes!

LAFITE OF FRENCH
In March 1976 struggling Southport, a Division Four club, signed Graham Lafite. He made two appearances before it was discovered that he had been playing under an assumed name. In reality he was Graham French, formerly with Shrewsbury Town, Swindon Town and Luton Town.

AGE OLD PROBLEM
Doncaster Rovers goalkeeper Ken Hardwick was chosen to play in the England Under-23 trial in January 1955. Then the Football Association discovered he was 30.

PHOTOGRAPHIC EVIDENCE
In 1967–68 Birmingham City dropped the idea of reproducing pictures of Blues players taking

penalty kicks following a miss by Malcolm Beard in the game against Blackpool. Their goalkeeper Alan Taylor took notice of the picture showing Beard scoring with a left-footed shot to the goalkeeper's right. Taylor chose the same way and Blackpool won 2–1.

TWO BREAKS

On 2 October 1970, the Italian international forward Luigi Riva broke a boy's arm with a shot during a practice game. On 31 October, Riva broke his own left leg playing for Italy against Austria in Vienna.

FATAL ERROR

Fulham goalkeeper Frank Elliot was playing at Plymouth Argyle on 2 October 1954. He challenged the Argyle centre-forward but hurt his back and fell to the ground injured, at the same time throwing the ball over his head and into the net for an own goal. Plymouth won 3–2.

RAVING VAN RAVENS

In 1971–72 Glasgow Rangers managed to win the Cup-Winners Cup but only after surviving a defeat in the second round. On 20 October 1971 they beat Sporting Lisbon 3–2 in the home leg but lost the return game on 3 November 4–3. This should have given them the tie on the away goals rule, but after the match, the referee Van Ravens ordered a penalty shoot-out. Three Rangers players had their shots saved, another missed the target and Sporting won the contest 2–0. But the official was later suspended and Rangers passed through on the away goals rule.

PING PONGED THEM IN
Schang Kun Ping scored six goals for South Korea against Thailand in an international in 1954.

PENGUIN WRAPPERS
Bolton Wanderers arrived at Middlesbrough railway station in the late 1940s only to discover that the player's shinguards were missing from the kit. Bill Ridding, the Bolton trainer, purchased 22 paperback romantic novels as temporary replacements.

ONE WAY TICKET
In May 1963 Arthur Lightening, Middlesbrough's goalkeeper, was given permission to return home to South Africa to attend his brother's wedding. He did not come back.

WE'LL CLAMP AGAIN
On 1 December Tottenham Hotspur stopped for lunch on the way to Stamford Bridge at the Royal Lancaster Hotel. Unfortunately they discovered after the meal that their coach had been towed away for illegal parking. It contained their kit. The missing equipment was eventually located but the kick-off at Chelsea had to be delayed ten minutes. Spurs lost 3–2. Terry Venables team were later fined £20000 – £15000 suspended – for their late arrival.

DOWN AND OUT
On 4 May 1935 Tottenham Hotspur lost 4–3 at Leeds United in a Division One match. Only 7668 turned up to watch the game. Spurs finished bottom and were relegated.

LING(ERING) DEFEAT
Referee Bill Ling gave West Germany a corner in the last few seconds of their game with the Republic of Ireland in Dublin on 17 October 1951 with the home side leading 3-2. The Germans headed an equaliser only to find it disallowed by Ling who had blown for full-time. Next day a German newspaper headline read: *GERMANY BEATEN 3–3 IN DUBLIN.*

IMPERATIVE PAIR OF TEETH
In April 1960 in Denmark, Norager were leading Ebeltoft 4–3. Referee Henning Erikstrup was about to blow for full-time when his dentures fell out. While he was recovering them, Ebeltoft equalised. The official disallowed the goal, replaced his false teeth and blew his whistle. Ebeltoft protested and Erikstrup admitted that his main concern had been to save his teeth before someone trod on them.

COLLECTOR'S ITEM
The last page of the Chelsea v Newcastle United match programme on 10 December 1955 had a footnote which read: 'Published for Arsenal Football Club Ltd'.

VOODOO HOODOO
During Oldham Athletic's 1967 tour of Rhodesia, local witch doctors were reported to have spread voodoo powers along the home teams' goal lines to prevent Oldham scoring. It was not successful. Oldham scored 45 goals in 11 games, only one of which was lost.

CIGGI-RATES
In 1991 the Bulgarian club Levski obtained sponsorship from an Italian company called Ciggi.

FOWL-MOUTHED
Bobby Fairfoul, who captained Liverpool Boys in 1920–21 and was capped at schoolboy level for England against Wales, was nicknamed 'chicken' or 'fairy'.

SEEKING GAME ELSEWHERE
In March 1927 Gateshead centre-half Cyril Hunter was suspended for four months. In April 1931 he was suspended for the whole of the 1931–32 season. He then emigrated to the USA.

OUTSIDE HELP
On 25 December 1954 Carlisle United beat Rochdale 7–2 in a Division Four match; their scorers included three own goals by Rochdale defenders.

JAWS TWO
On 19 August 1975, Alex Stepney the Manchester United goalkeeper was taken to hospital during an away game with Birmingham City with a dislocated jaw, sustained by apparently shouting at a team-mate.

BROWN'S BACK TROUBLE
Amateur goalkeeper Fred Brown was playing for Aldershot reserves against Millwall reserves at The Den on 15 March 1952. Twice he drop-kicked the ball against the back of Millwall forward Jimmy Constantine and both times the ball rebounded into the goal. Aldershot lost 4–1. Brown did go on to better times, turning professional with the club and later playing for West Bromwich Albion and Portsmouth.

SUICIDAL TENDENCIES
On Boxing Day 1952, Sheffield Wednesday lost 5–4 to West Bromwich Albion, conceding three own goals in the process.

DAY OF THE 'STIFF' HEADS
On the opening day of the 1954–55 season, John Crawford, centre-half for Dunfermline Athletic reserves, conceded a penalty and put through his own goal twice in a 5–2 defeat at home to the Montrose 'Stiffs'.

MANY A SLIP . . .
After Charlton Athletic won the FA Cup in 1947, manager Jimmy Seed dropped the trophy and broke the top off the lid. A garage made temporary repairs before a Town Hall reception, after which a silversmith completed a professional job.

CREWE ALL AT SEA
Crewe Alexandra won only three of their first 57 away fixtures in the Football League from 1892–93 in Division Two. These included three seasons in which they failed to win any away games.

KIT BAGGED
On 21 October 1989 Newcastle United left Brighton after a 3–0 Division Two win at the Goldstone Ground with just one unreported casualty. As the team's kit baskets were being unloaded at the hotel, the wind caught hold of the trolley and dispatched it on a sight-seeing trip down the promenade. Alas it met a number 67 bus heading in the opposite direction.

BAR TO PROMOTION
In 1908–09 West Bromwich Albion missed promotion by one fifty-sixth of a goal. At Blackpool they were robbed by a referee's decision when Charlie Hewitt's shot hit the underside of the crossbar and rebounded. Bill Garraty their centre-forward was so sure it was a goal he did not bother to tap the ball into the net.

COACH OFF THE RAILS
Because of an injury crisis at Bournemouth, club coach Harry Redknapp was forced to play himself against Manchester United on 6 October 1982 in a Milk Cup second round first leg game at Old Trafford. He had not played a senior game for four and a half years. He put through his own goal after 28 minutes and United won 2–0. Exactly a month later Bournemouth manager David Webb had to turn out for his first game in two years in a League game against Huddersfield Town. He took himself off after 68 minutes in a 1–0 defeat. A month later Webb was sacked.

STRIKING PARTNERSHIPS
Mike Flanagan and Derek Hales were colleagues in two separate spells at Charlton Athletic, but there was tension between the two during the second period of their acquaintanceship. In an FA Cup third round tie at home against Maidstone United on 9 January 1979, the two were involved in an exchange of blows and were sent off by referee Brian Martin five minutes before the end of the game.

CARELESS HANDS
On 17 October 1925 Aston Villa were leading Birmingham 3–0 with ten minutes to play. Thousands had already started to drift homewards. Then Joe Bradford struck two goals for Birmingham and set up an exciting finish. Charlie Spiers, the Aston Villa goalkeeper, in attempting to clear an attack, managed to throw the ball into his own net for the equaliser.

RODGERS AND OUT
David Rodgers of Bristol City scored in four successive Division One matches in 1978–79. On 26 August he scored the only goal of the game at home to Aston Villa. The following week at Wolverhampton he put through his own goal as Wolves won 2–0. On 9 September another own goal cost them the game at Tottenham Hotspur and on 16 September he scored one for City in a 3–1 win over Southampton.

SHEEPISH CLOTHING
On 15 August 1973 a Sunday League amateur side played against Mainz, West Germany, mistakenly billed as Wolverhampton. Locals put out their strongest side, thinking the opposition to be Wolves. Mainz won 21–0.

One hat-trick unpopular with the (Ms) Bill

HULLO, HULLO

Playing for Blackburn Rovers in a Simod Cup second round tie against Sunderland on 22 December 1988 at Ewood Park, Colin Hendry went to retrieve the ball which had gone out of play. It ran towards a policewoman and Hendry thought for a bit of fun to knock her hat over her eyes. Unfortunately it completely flew off her head and he received a stern warning.

VIEW FROM THE BRIDGE

On 26 September 1970 in a Division One match between Chelsea and Ipswich Town at Stamford Bridge, Chelsea's Alan Hudson sent in a shot at an angle which struck the side netting and rebounded into play. Referee Roy Capey signalled a goal and despite protests from Ipswich players and subsequently by the club, the result, a 2–1 win for Chelsea, was allowed to stand.

DUNN ROAMING

On 26 April 1950 Jimmy Dunn was playing right-back for Leeds United against Blackburn Rovers at Elland Road. He hit a long ball into the opponents' penalty area, it bounced through one defender's legs, through another's and into the net. It was to be the only goal he scored in 443 League and Cup games for the club.

GETTING SHIRTY

Eddie Kelly threw his shirt at the trainer's bench when he was substituted by Arsenal against Leicester City on 8 September 1973 in a 2–0 defeat. Three days later at the start of the match with Sheffield United, he came onto the field minus his shirt. He then pulled on the number 11 jersey. Arsenal won 1–0.

NEWPORT'S LATE START

Newport County hold the record for the worst start to a season by a League club. By 19 December 1970 they had completed 23 matches without a win, overhauling Bolton Wanderers record set up in 1903. On 15 January 1971 Newport beat Southend United 3–0 in their 26th game of the season. It was their first win since 25 April 1970.

TRANSFERS
OF DELIGHT

JULIAN THE SIXTH

Between November and February during the 1989–90 season, Julian Broddle played under six different League club managers. At Barnsley Allan Clarke was sacked, Eric Winstanley took over as caretaker until Mel Machin was appointed. Broddle was transferred to Plymouth Argyle in January for £80000, and played under Ken Brown until he was sacked and John Gregory took over as caretaker. Number six was David Kemp.

SMART SVARC

Bobby Svarc was a Lincoln City player on loan to Barrow. But Lincoln did not want him cup-tied, so he was recalled. On 21 November 1970, in an FA Cup first round match, he played against Barrow and scored in a 2–1 win.

THE MAN FROM UNCLE

In March 1949 the £23850 fee paid by Derby County to Manchester United made Johnny Morris the game's highest-priced player at the time. But Eddie Quigley, his uncle, overtook him in the following December when he left Sheffield Wednesday for Preston North End in a £26500 move.

ALL THREE CODES

Ben Beynon began as a Welsh rugby union player before joining Swansea Town as a centre-forward. He went back to rugby, playing for Wales as stand-off half against Scotland on 7 February 1920. Seven days later he was heading the Swansea attack. He then turned professional with Oldham Rugby League club but in August 1926 went back to Swansea for the third time.

WRIGHTON MARCH

Frank Wrighton, a Sheldon born forward, moved three times in mid-March during the 1930s. In 1930 he was transferred from Darlington to Manchester City; in 1932 from City to Fulham and the following year from Fulham to Exeter City.

STAR TREK

Third Lanark transferred ten players to English clubs in the space of a year up to 1963: Alex Harley and Matt Gray (Manchester City), Dave Hilley (Newcastle United), Jimmy Robb (Charlton Athletic), David Grant and Peter Kerr (Reading), Willie Clarkson (Oxford United), John McLaughlin (Shrewsbury Town), Robbie Stenhouse (Crewe Alexandra) and Gavin Fletcher (Bradford City).

OLD WOLVES HOME

Twenty-three players who had all been with Wolverhampton Wanderers at sometime or another ended up at Bournemouth in the 1930s: Adkins, Akers, Bellis, Bird, Bucknall, Burgin, Burns, Farrow, Flaherty, Harvey, Kirkham,

Langley, Lovery, Marsden, Mordue, Morgan, Pincott, Sellars, Smith, Taylor, Twiss, Whittam and Wilson.

THAT'S YOUR LOT

Billy Lot Jones made his final League appearance for Wrexham at the age of 46 in 1921–22. His lengthy career had taken him from Chirk and Druids to Manchester City, then Southend United, Aberdare, Wrexham, Oswestry and then back to Chirk as player-manager. He was capped 20 times by Wales and usually figured at inside-left. When Billy Meredith's sports shop went into bankruptcy in 1909, he was one of the creditors.

'Lot' number one: a pair of boots

HARTLEY HARE

Gateshead born Tom Hartley, who had played for his local Football League side in pre-war days, was involved with five clubs in five months during 1947–48. An inside-forward, he was on Chesterfield's transfer list at the time. In September he joined Stockton, North Shields in December and Leicester City three weeks later on 1 January. On January 28 he became one of five Leicester players – Calvert, Cheney, Eggleston and Osborne were the others – who were transferred to Watford.

CHRISTMAS PRESENT

Harry Lovatt played for Leicester City Reserves against Coventry City Reserves in the London Combination on Christmas Day 1930. That evening he was transferred to Notts County and led their attack next day against Coventry in Division Three (South).

RARELY SEEN GILZEAN

While serving in the RASC on National Service, Alan Gilzean played on loan to Aldershot from Dundee during 1958–59. But he played chiefly in the A team, scoring more than 20 goals, and had a few reserve games, yet did not figure once in the League side.

FAMILY MOVES

In September 1946 former Oldham Athletic and England goalkeeper Jack Hacking, then Accrington Stanley manager, transferred his own son, Jack Hacking jnr, also a goalkeeper, to Stockport County. In the 1990 close-season manager Ian Bowyer left Hereford United by mutual consent after a disagreement following his failure to sign his own son Gary on a contract and allowing him to join Nottingham Forest.

BIBLE PUNCHER

In 1991 the Mexico City club America signed Antonio Dos Santos a 26-year-old striker from the El Salvador club Luis Angel Firpo. A Brazilian he was also an evangelist preacher who played under the name of Biblico.

FROM GLENN MILLER TO A ROLLING STONE

South African born Steve Mokone became the rolling stone of world soccer in the early 1960s. In seven years he played for Coventry City, Heracles (Holland), Cardiff City, Benfica (Portugal), Barnsley, Salisbury United (Southern Rhodesia), Torino (Italy) and Hamilton Steelers (Canada). He turned professional with Coventry in October 1956 after Charlie Buchan's *Football Monthly* magazine contributed £100 to his fare. He was nicknamed 'Kalamazoo' as he was always whistling the tune from the Glenn Miller Film *Orchestra Wives*.

FLOATING SHARES

In 1953 Moat Villa, an Ellesmere Port junior team, received a football from Everton in exchange for Colin Evans who then went into Everton's 'C' team.

STOCK EXCHANGE

In June 1955 Sheffield Wednesday and Huddersfield Town were involved in a major transfer deal in which two players from each side joined the other club without money changing hands. Tony Conwell and Jackie Marriott moved from Wednesday to Huddersfield, Ron Staniforth and Roy Shiner moved in the opposite direction.

EE AY ADEY OH!

Arthur Adey, a centre-forward, played for eight different clubs in just over five years between 1950 and 1955: Bishop Auckland, Doncaster Rovers, Gillingham, Bradford Park Avenue, Bedford Town, Worcester City, Chelmsford City and Rugby Town.

POST EARLY

On Boxing Day 1972, the Blackburn Rovers v Chesterfield match had to be replayed because Chesterfield fielded an ineligible player in goalkeeper Jim Brown. He had been transferred to them on 22 December, but the letter to the Football League was held up in the Christmas post, arriving two days later.

KEELEY MOVES

In October 1947 Accrington Stanley transferred inside-left Walter Keeley to Port Vale for a record fee. In September 1948 Port Vale transferred him back to Accrington for their record amount.

FINGER LICKIN' MOVE

In November 1985 Bangor City agreed to transfer part-time centre-forward Vivian Williams, a frozen-chicken packer, to Atletico Madrid for £25 000.

NO STAYING POWER

Carlisle United loaned Frank Sharp to Southport in February 1969, recalled him on 18 February and transferred him to Cardiff City on 19 February. Steve Sherwood left Chelsea for Fulham on loan one Tuesday in 1976–77 and was sold to Watford the following Friday. On 16 February 1990 Steve Anthrobus was transferred from Millwall to Wimbledon. Seven days earlier he had gone on loan to Southend United only to be brought back four days later.

POUND OF FLESH

On 29 January 1975 Huddersfield Town transferred Paul Smith to Cambridge United for £1.

FOOTBALL LEAGUE OF NATIONS

In the 1990–91 season, the Football League had 40 foreigners playing in the competition, excluding players from the Republic of Ireland. It was possible to field two complete teams from 22 different countries.

CRAIG FORREST (Ipswich Town) . . . . Canada

JOHN HARKES (Sheffield Wednesday) . . . . USA

CHRIS ZORICICH (Leyton Orient) . . . . . New Zealand

RAY ATTEVELD (Everton) . . . . Holland

ERLAND JOHNSEN (Chelsea) . . . . Norway

KENT NIELSEN (Aston Villa) . . . . Denmark

DWIGHT YORKE (Aston Villa) . . . . Trinidad

CHARLIE NTAMARK (Walsall) . . . . Cameroon

RONNIE ROSENTHAL (Liverpool) . . . . Israel

ROY WEGERLE (QPR) . . . . South Africa

NAYIM (Tottenham Hotspur) . . . . Spain

and

BRUCE GROBBELAAR (Liverpool) . . . . Zimbabwe

ALEK CHEREDNIK (Southampton) . . . . USSR

GUDNI BERGSSON (Tottenham Hotspur) . . . . Iceland

JOHN BUTTIGIEG (Brentford) . . . . Malta

NESTOR LORENZO (Swindon Town) . . . . . Argentina

STEFAN IOVAN (Brighton) . . . . Romania

IVO STAS (Aston Villa) . . . . Czechoslovakia

THOMAS HAUSER (Sunderland) . . . . Germany

ROBERT WARZYCHA (Everton) . . . . Poland

DOMINIC IORFA (QPR) . . . . Nigeria

ANDERS LIMPAR (Arsenal) . . . . Sweden

THAT'S FINAL

HIGH COURT LOW
Before the 1983 FA Cup Final, Brighton & Hove Albion captain Steve Foster had reached 31 disciplinary points and was to be banned from the match. He decided to take his plea to the High Court but lost. In his absence Brighton drew 2–2 with Manchester United. He came back at centre-half for the replay which Brighton lost 4–0.

DOUBLING-UP
In the 1931 FA Cup Final the opposing goalkeepers Harry Hibbs (Birmingham) and Hubert Pearson (West Bromwich Albion) were both products of Tamworth Castle FC. The following year Newcastle United's goalkeeper Albert McInroy and Arsenal's Frank Moss both came from the Preston area.

LEAVE ALONE
Vivian Woodward obtained leave from the Army to play in the 1915 FA Cup Final for Chelsea against Sheffield United. But Bob Thomson had played in every previous round, scoring six goals in seven matches. Though Thomson was prepared to drop out, Woodward insisted he stay in and declined a place. But Sheffield United won 3–0.

ALL THAT GLITTERS . . .
William Gildea played centre-half for Bradford City against Newcastle United, a goalless FA Cup Final at Crystal Palace in 1911 but his place was taken in the replay by Robert Torrance, who received a winners' medal after City's 1–0 win while Gildea missed out on one himself.

UNCHANGED MELODY
In 1959 both FA Cup finalists, Nottingham Forest and Luton Town, were unchanged throughout the competition.

RULE RIDICULE
On 5 May 1982, Mixenden '76 were beaten 1–0 in the Halifax and District FA Dunkley Cup Final by Golden Fleece. They had to turn out a ten-man team because the rules of the competition prevented them from including two players who had not taken part in earlier rounds.

TARTAN FLAVOUR
In the 1937 FA Cup Final there were 12 Scots on the field, seven of them with Preston North End, five with Sunderland.

VARYING MAGPIES
Newcastle United's 1952 FA Cup-winning team comprised four Englishmen, three Scots, two Chileans (the Robledo brothers), one Irishman and a Welshman.

DOUBLE DEBIT ENTRY
Bob Barclay played in two FA Cup finals for different clubs in three seasons but lost both times, first for Sheffield United against Arsenal in 1936, then Huddersfield Town against Preston North End 1938.

WHISTLER'S BOTHER

For the first time in 1966 the referee for the FA Cup Final collected a fee. Previously the official had been given the choice of a medal or a fee. Everyone had taken the medal. From 1966 they had both.

THREE TIME LOSER

Pat Beasley missed playing in Arsenal's unsuccessful 1932 FA Cup Final team and again in 1936 after playing in all rounds up to the final. After that game, Alex James offered him his winner's medal which he declined with thanks. But in 1938 he made it with Huddersfield Town, although they were beaten.

ABSENTEE AWARDS

Two Aston Villa players, Albert Allen and Harold Edgley, each received FA Cup winners' medals, although neither played in the Final that year. Allen was injured and missed the 1887 game after appearing in every round. Edgley missed the 1920 Final after breaking his leg at Stamford Bridge in a League match three weeks before Villa met Huddersfield Town on the same ground. Edgley's gold medal had the inscription: 'Reserve Man'.

FRANK'S NAP ENDS NIGHTMARE

Frank McLintock played in five Wembley finals but had to wait until the fifth before finishing on the winning side. In 1961 and 1963 he had been in Leicester City's beaten side in the FA Cup, and was in Arsenal's runners-up teams of 1968 and 1969 in the League Cup. Then in 1971 he captained Arsenal's successful FA Cup winning side as they completed their League and Cup double.

VILLA VISTA

In 1913 Aston Villa won the FA Cup, scoring 20 goals and conceding just one on the way. In the final they beat Sunderland 1–0 and it was the first time in the history of the competition that the top two clubs in the country had contested the game. Sunderland were League champions, Villa runners-up. This was also the first final in which a penalty was missed.

STAN THE MAN

Stan Seymour, who scored one of Newcastle United's goals in their 2–0 win over Aston Villa in the 1924 FA Cup Final, had had earlier experience across the border. During the War Shield of 1914–15 he was in Morton's successful team which beat Rangers 2–1 in the final of that competition.

BLANK VERSE

On 14 January 1914 an 'In Memoriam' card was produced in Bristol for the Cup replay with Queen's Park Rangers. It read: 'In Brightful memory of Queen's Park R. Football Team, who were beaten in the re-play of the First Round of the English Cup, at Bristol, by Bristol City, on Wednesday, Jan 14th 1914.

> Queen's Park is a clever Team, there's not the slightest doubt,
> But Bristol City fairly knocked them out;
> They were determined to win, or at least to have a try,
> But now they have to wait till the sweet bye-and-bye.
> Never count your Chickens till they are hatched.'

Alas, it was all in vain. QPR won 2–0 after extra time.